The First Crusade

A Brief History with Documents

THE BEDFORD SERIES IN HISTORY AND CULTURE

The First Crusade

A Brief History with Documents

Jay Rubenstein

University of Tennessee–Knoxville

BEDFORD / ST. MARTIN'S Boston ◆ New York

To Phil Niles, Bob Bonner, and Carl Weiner

For Bedford/St. Martin's

Vice President, Editorial, Macmillan Higher Education Humanities: Edwin Hill
Publisher for History: Michael Rosenberg
Senior Executive Editor for History: William J. Lombardo
Director of Development for History: Jane Knetzger
Developmental Editor: Danielle Slevens
Editorial Assistant: Arrin Kaplan
Assistant Production Editor: Lidia MacDonald-Carr
Production Associate: Victoria Anzalone
Executive Marketing Manager: Sandra McGuire
Project Management: Books By Design, Inc.
Copy Editor: Barbara Jatkola
Cartography: Mapping Specialists, Ltd.
Director of Rights and Permissions: Hilary Newman
Senior Art Director: Anna Palchik
Text Design: Claire Seng-Niemoeller
Cover Design: William Boardman
Cover Art: Yates Thompson 12 f.29 Battle scene outside Antioch, ca. 1098, from Estoire d'Outremer (vellum), William of Tyre (ca. 1130–1185)/British Library, London, UK/ © British Library Board. All Rights Reserved/Bridgeman Images.
Composition: Achorn International, Inc.
Printing and Binding: RR Donnelley and Sons

For information, write: Bedford / St. Martin's, 75 Arlington Street, Boston, MA 02116 (617-399-4000)

ISBN 978-1-4576-2910-5

Acknowledgments

Text acknowledgments and copyrights appear at the back of the book on page 170, which constitutes an extension of the copyright page. Art acknowledgments and copyrights appear on the same page as the art selections they cover. It is a violation of the law to reproduce these selections by any means whatsoever without the written permission of the copyright holder.

Foreword

The Bedford Series in History and Culture is designed so that readers can study the past as historians do.

The historian's first task is finding the evidence. Documents, letters, memoirs, interviews, pictures, movies, novels, or poems can provide facts and clues. Then the historian questions and compares the sources. There is more to do than in a courtroom, for hearsay evidence is welcome, and the historian is usually looking for answers beyond act and motive. Different views of an event may be as important as a single verdict. How a story is told may yield as much information as what it says.

Along the way the historian seeks help from other historians and perhaps from specialists in other disciplines. Finally, it is time to write, to decide on an interpretation and how to arrange the evidence for readers.

Each book in this series contains an important historical document or group of documents, each document a witness from the past and open to interpretation in different ways. The documents are combined with some element of historical narrative—an introduction or a biographical essay, for example—that provides students with an analysis of the primary source material and important background information about the world in which it was produced.

Each book in the series focuses on a specific topic within a specific historical period. Each provides a basis for lively thought and discussion about several aspects of the topic and the historian's role. Each is short enough (and inexpensive enough) to be a reasonable one-week assignment in a college course. Whether as classroom or personal reading, each book in the series provides firsthand experience of the challenge—and fun—of discovering, recreating, and interpreting the past.

Lynn Hunt
David W. Blight
Bonnie G. Smith
Natalie Zemon Davis

Preface

The First Crusade (1095–1099) was, arguably, the pivotal event in the Middle Ages and one of the central events in world history. Jerusalem's conquest in 1099 brought Europeans into closer contact with Arab, Byzantine, and Asian cultures and created in Europe itself a new sense of a common identity and a shared cultural achievement. It also raises troubling and important historical and humanistic questions about the place of religious violence in the development of Western and world history, with a specific focus on the city of Jerusalem, still the most fiercely contested spiritual and geographic spot on earth. This volume seeks to explore both the particular events of the First Crusade and the larger implications of this sudden incursion of medieval European culture into the Middle Eastern world.

Part one lays out a fundamental contention of this volume: that historians cannot understand the reasons behind the First Crusade if they do not take seriously the religious motives of the participants. At the same time, the introduction helps students to recognize that those religious motivations were very different from what modern practice might lead them to expect. In the Middle Ages, both Christianity and Islam were faiths rooted in ritual practice, historical memory, and geographic location. Each religion also professed ideals of peace, even as many of its adherents actively embraced the profession of war. The introduction emphasizes the critical importance of Jerusalem in both religions, given its history and its prophetic associations. For Christians in particular, Jerusalem was not just the birthplace of their faith. It was also the symbol of heaven on earth. In the eleventh century, as the introduction makes clear, European Christians became increasingly worried about the state of Jerusalem. Rumors of atrocities committed there by Muslims made that rival faith's possession of the city seem increasingly intolerable. The eventual response from the West was a massive military campaign, proclaimed by the pope and by street preachers alike. This campaign's unlikely success, the introduction explains, had profoundly transformative effects on Christianity, Islam, politics, and culture in East and West.

The documents in part two provide a rich variety of both Christian and Muslim perspectives, allowing students to analyze the crusade through the words of those who experienced, chronicled, imagined, and reacted to it. Students will meet some of the key personalities in the war and will be able to discuss what motivated warriors to "take the cross" (literally, to have crosses sewn onto their clothing as a sign of their intention to march to Jerusalem). Through a series of letters and historical narratives written around the time of the crusade (by Latin, Greek, and Arabic writers), as well as images of some of the art and architecture that both shaped and reflected the spirit of the crusade, readers will be able to evaluate what motivated the events, from the chaotic response to the initial sermons right down to the final bloody battle before and atop the walls of Jerusalem. Not just an exercise in military history, the documents and visuals specially chosen for this volume cast light on the brutal realities of the conflict and the apparent bizarre miracles that regularly punctuated the march.

Document headnotes, a detailed chronology, and a map indicating major sites, battles, and crusader routes provide students with the context they need to understand what they are reading. A list of Questions for Consideration at the end of the volume points both teachers and students toward engaging, controversial topics for discussion or writing assignments. Finally, a bibliography of primary and secondary sources, categorized by topic, allows students to undertake their own further research on the questions raised here. All translations of Latin material are the author's own. Others translators are acknowledged as appropriate.

ACKNOWLEDGMENTS

This book owes its existence to the initial encouragement of Professor Lynn Hunt and of Mary Dougherty at Bedford/St. Martin's. Danielle Slevens carefully edited the entire manuscript, and Jane Knetzger, Heidi Hood, Laura Kintz, and Arrin Kaplan provided invaluable support throughout the editorial process, as did my graduate student Trevor Myers. Thanks to Lidia MacDonald-Carr and Nancy Benjamin, who ably handled production, and to copy editor Barbara Jatkola. My agent, Deborah Grosvenor, took care of all the professional details that otherwise leave me baffled. My wonderful wife and frequent editor, Meredith

McGroarty, always makes my writing better. Thanks are due as well to Will Fontanez, the director of the Cartographic Services Laboratory at the University of Tennessee, for providing expert advice on the map that appears in this book. And finally I must thank the small army of outside evaluators who read an early draft of the manuscript: David Bachrach, University of New Hampshire; Steven Isaac, Longwood University; Amy Livingstone, Wittenberg University; Mark Pegg, Washington University in St. Louis; Jarbel Rodriguez, San Francisco State University; and Brett Whalen, University of North Carolina at Chapel Hill.

Working on a book like this one inevitably made me think of my own undergraduate teachers, and it is to them that I would like to dedicate this volume: to Phil Niles, Bob Bonner, and Carl Weiner, who are still my heroes.

Jay Rubenstein

Contents

APPENDIXES

Map and Illustrations

MAP

ILLUSTRATIONS

PART ONE

Introduction: Christianity, Islam, and the Beginning of the Crusades

In the autumn and winter of 1095–1096, Pope Urban II and others—a hermit named Peter, a warrior called Emicho of Flonheim, and an unnamed woman who believed that God had infused her goose with the Holy Spirit—all began to proclaim a radical idea: that Christians needed to go to the Middle East and wage war against Islam with the goal of recapturing Jerusalem. European Christians had fought earlier wars against Muslims. The Franks had famously defeated armies of the Umayyad Caliphate near the French city of Poitiers in 732. Closer in time to the crusade, eleventh-century Norman mercenaries had fought against Islamic principalities in southern Italy and Sicily. Christian soldiers in Spain were simultaneously campaigning against Muslims in the Iberian Peninsula, a conflict that would last for centuries and that historians would eventually name the Reconquista. But these hostilities were more about land than religion. The First Crusade (1096–1099) was something different. It created a new military ethos, one that melded a warrior's brutality with the penitential ideals of a clergyman and the apocalyptic sensibilities of a street preacher.

The First Crusade also set a pattern. According to tradition, there were a total of eight crusades in the Middle Ages, and the presence of French-speaking Christian settlements in the Middle East from 1099 to 1291 meant that Christian-Muslim combat became something of a way of life for both sides. The First Crusade thus had a long afterlife. The ethos of crusading also expanded into other theaters of combat—into Iberia against Muslims, the Baltics against pagans, and southern France against heretics. Most notoriously, the Fourth Crusade (1202–1204), through a series of financial missteps and ill-advised political alliances, culminated with the devastation of the capital of Byzantium, Constantinople, the Greek-speaking successor state of the Roman Empire. The 1204 sack of Constantinople has attained an infamous reputation for its savagery, but it was surely no more a crime against humanity than the battles fought at Antioch and Jerusalem during the First Crusade.

Rather than try to encapsulate the many different aspects of all the medieval crusades, this book focuses instead on the point of origin, the First Crusade. It was this war that set the pattern for its successors. The First Crusade—an achievement shared across cultural, geographic, and linguistic boundaries—was the epic that defined the medieval West. An army of tens of thousands of warriors with no single leader, united only by religious fervor, journeyed two thousand miles to Jerusalem, along the way triumphing again and again over numerically superior enemies. Before the fighting ended, at least two of the participants were already writing books about it. These chroniclers, like the hundreds of historians who have succeeded them, recognized that they were facing a topic of huge significance and equally great mystery. In just three years, the crusade had changed the direction of warfare, religion, and perhaps history itself. How and why had this happened?

HOLY WAR

A contemporary historian named Guibert of Nogent (ca. 1060–ca. 1125) viewed the First Crusade as both "a new path to salvation" and "a new type of war." God had created in his days "holy battles" that allowed laymen to redeem their sins and enter heaven.[1] It was the first real example of holy war in the medieval era, a war fought in the name of God, where the slaughter of the enemy was not a regrettable, unavoidable consequence of combat but was instead a sign of virtue—the more vicious the warrior, the more focused upon mayhem, the more honorable his service. And if a warrior should happen to die on the battlefield, he would surely attain salvation, like martyrs in the days of the early church. Salvation history was, in this respect, repeating itself; the same writer, Guibert of Nogent, celebrated the crusade because it had inaugurated "a new age of martyrs."[2]

These characteristics together—a religious goal, the direct intervention of God, sanctified violence, and a belief that the dead in battle were martyrs—define a holy war. It is a sadly familiar concept in our world, accustomed as we are to the religious rhetoric of suicide bombers who earnestly believe that acts of destruction (and self-destruction) will earn them a place in paradise. Though familiar to us, "holy war" was an unfamiliar concept in eleventh-century Europe. Warfare was simply a necessary evil, with an emphasis on the word *evil.* Consider, for example, the Norman Conquest of England in 1066. Duke William of Normandy invaded England because he claimed that it was his rightful inheritance. Before launching the attack, he sought the blessing of Pope Alexander II, who endorsed William's cause and sent him a papal banner to carry into battle. Nonetheless, after William's victory, a papal representative imposed penance on all the victorious soldiers for every violent act committed in combat. Even in what was—theoretically, at least—a clear-cut example of a just war, a campaign to claim property unjustly taken from the invading army's leader, warfare remained a sin.

Regardless of circumstance, then, violence was seen much as it is today—as a social problem. To control it, bishops around the year 1000 had sought to impose on Europe's erratic warrior class a peace, usually called the Peace of God. To implement this plan, bishops would gather into one location all the major relics—usually, saints' bones—in their dioceses and then ask the soldiers living under their spiritual authority to swear before these relics to keep the peace. In essence, warriors agreed not to attack the unarmed (churchmen, merchants, women, and peasants) and to respect the sanctuary of church grounds. In the 1020s, bishops attempted to create a more restrictive agreement, the Truce of God, in which warriors would swear to limit violent acts to certain days of the week. The success of these movements is uncertain, but they do lead to one important conclusion: Churchmen in the eleventh century were unable to define warfare, the central activity of the men who in fact governed society, in a positive fashion. An essential part of everyday life (and one that churchmen were perfectly willing to exploit when it suited their goals), war nonetheless had no intellectually defensible role to play in the Christian world.

In this respect, the First Crusade created an ethical revolution. Violence committed on the road to Jerusalem was not only permissible but also virtuous. A warrior could even win himself a place in heaven by actively killing Christ's enemies. Christian doctrine offers no support for this belief. Christ had told Roman soldiers to be content with their wages.[3] He had not instructed them to use their powers to kill wicked men. To find a doctrine of holy war, clerics turned from the New Testament to the Old, in which God's chosen people, the Israelites, regularly fought in his name. An abstract theory of how to behave in combat appears in the Mosaic book of Deuteronomy (see Document 1). Churchmen could also teach proper military behavior through Old Testament stories, such as the war between the Israelites and the Amalekites. After an extremely brutal victory, King Saul failed to follow God's instructions to the letter (see Document 2) and lost all of his authority as a result. At least one twelfth-century historian cited this story as a precedent for the crusaders' decision to slaughter the entire Muslim garrison at Jerusalem.[4] That kind of borrowing from the Old Testament was not unprecedented. Medieval European notions of kingship, for example, were based explicitly on Jewish practice. On a more theoretical plane, European Christians had long viewed themselves as "the new Israel," not just the successors to the Israelites, but the people who had displaced them in God's plan for salvation. Rules of war, therefore, could be found in the Bible, though clerics needed to read widely and to pick and choose in order to assemble them.

Islam, by contrast, had a highly developed theory of religious warfare. The usual term for a Muslim holy war is a *jihad*, which translates literally as "struggle." According to a tradition outside the Qur'an, the Islamic holy book, the Prophet Muhammad divided jihad into two categories: the greater jihad, which is an internal, spiritual struggle, and the lesser jihad, which is straightforward combat. Regardless of the historicity of this tradition, Muhammad's world was one in which small-scale battles—similar to what eleventh-century Europeans would have been familiar with—were normal. The most important Islamic rules for combat appear in Surah 8 of the Qur'an (see Document 3), called "The Spoils of War." More detailed and practical than the Old Testament stories and strictures, the rules in the Qur'an were nonetheless intended for a tribal desert society, not for the sophisticated and far-flung civilization that Islam became in the century after Muhammad's death (632 CE).

JERUSALEM

Arguably the most consequential of Islam's early conquests was the capture of Jerusalem in the year 637. By that time, Jerusalem had been a Christian city for over three centuries (except for a fifteen-year period when the Persian Empire controlled it). Christians of all traditions revered Jerusalem as the place where Christ had been crucified and resurrected, but it was no longer the city of the Bible. In 70 CE, Roman soldiers had destroyed much of the ancient city, including the temple structure built by King Herod. Other Roman soldiers leveled Jerusalem altogether during the Jewish revolt of 115–117 CE. Subsequently, the emperor Hadrian (r. 117–138) had an entirely new city built atop the ruins and named it Aelia Capitolina. The once great Jewish capital had become an insignificant imperial outpost.

It might have stayed that way, except that two centuries later the Roman emperor Constantine converted to Christianity, and as part of his transformative program for the empire, he sought to restore Jerusalem and to make it into a great religious capital. His mother, St. Helena, famously visited the city in 326–328 and helped plan the construction of a massive new temple complex, the Church of the Holy Sepulcher, purportedly built at the site of Christ's crucifixion and burial. According to legend, St. Helena directed archaeological digs that eventually led to the discovery of Christ's tomb and the secret location of the relic of the True Cross, on which Christ had been crucified. Jerusalem had been—appropriately enough—resurrected, but now as a thoroughly Roman and Christian city.

When the armies of Caliph Umar captured Jerusalem in 637 CE, they radically transformed its religious character and appearance. But they left the Christian monuments in place. Because Christians, like Jews, were part of the Abrahamic religious tradition, Muslims granted them special status and protection.[5] In practical terms, they could continue to live in Jerusalem and follow their faith. One of their monuments, the great domed Church of the Holy Sepulcher, dominated Jerusalem's skyline in 637. By the end of the seventh century, however, two new buildings overshadowed it: the Dome of the Rock and al-Aqsa Mosque. These two enormous edifices were built opposite each other on the highest ground in the city, the Temple Mount (called by Muslims Haram al-Sharif, or "Noble Sanctuary"), where the great Temple of Herod had once stood. They still dominate Jerusalem today.

The decision to build the Dome of the Rock and al-Aqsa Mosque on the old Temple Mount had spiritual as well as secular implications. Jerusalem, and in particular the Haram al-Sharif, were believed to be the site of Muhammad's Mi'raj, where he ascended into heaven (see Document 4). According to Islamic tradition, in the year 621 the Prophet, led by the angel Gabriel, rode the heavenly steed Buraq on a mystical journey that took him from Mecca to Jerusalem, and thence to heaven. The story is mentioned only obliquely in the Qur'an (17:1), where we read that Muhammad traveled from the sacred mosque (Mecca) to an unnamed "far mosque." Jerusalem was obviously not in 621 a place of Muslim worship, but it was nonetheless the most important (and from Mecca, the most distant) holy site with monotheistic, Abrahamic associations. The Dome of the Rock was built as a monument to Muhammad's journey, called the Night Journey. Al-Aqsa Mosque, whose name literally means "far mosque," stands in the place of whatever religious monument may have existed there during Muhammad's life.

Because of these associations with the Prophet's life, Jerusalem became a place of Islamic pilgrimage (see Documents 5 and 6). But it was also important to Muslims because for the first thirteen years of Islamic history, Jerusalem had been the *qibla*, the direction in which Muslims prayed. After the *qibla* was changed to Mecca, Jerusalem remained one of the three most sacred places in Islam—a point of history that probably none of the crusaders would have known. Indeed, the earliest crusader travel guide to Jerusalem does not even acknowledge the existence of either the Dome of the Rock or al-Aqsa Mosque (see Document 7). In the crusader imagination, Jerusalem was still very much a place of Christian pilgrimage, one barely changed from the days of Constantine and his archaeologically inclined mother. Much of the material in this twelfth-century guidebook, in fact, was drawn from a text written in the fourth century, over three hundred years before the advent of Islam.

As this observation suggests, the Middle East had grown largely unfamiliar to Western pilgrims. It was a powerful symbol of heaven on earth, but it was also a distant, almost impossible destination. Maps of Jerusalem from the time of the crusade bear minimal resemblance to the actual place. They usually represent it as an idealized, perfectly circular city filled with places of Christian worship (see Document 8). For the typical European Christian, during the years 600 to 1000, the allegorical Jerusalem—the Jerusalem that could be found in any church or in the peaceful heart of a true believer—had to suffice. And for most Christians during those years, that imaginary Jerusalem was indeed enough.

A few Christians, however, did maintain an interest in another aspect of Jerusalem's identity—as a city of prophecy, the place where the last battle of Armageddon would occur. It was a dangerous topic for speculation. On the one hand, the Bible clearly states that no one knows or can know the hour and the day of the end-time. On the other hand, often in the same passages, the Bible sets out signs by which Christians might recognize the Last Days.[6] Pulled in these contradictory directions, medieval writers and readers still sought answers to their questions about the fulfillment of the book of Revelation. They looked to the Bible, and they also wrote entirely new books of prophecy. Probably the most influential of them is attributed to an early theologian named Methodius (d. 311). Because the attribution is false, historians usually call the author of this book Pseudo-Methodius (see Document 9).

Pseudo-Methodius actually lived in the late seventh century, nearly four hundred years after the real Methodius had died. He wrote in response to Islam's rapid expansion, at a time when Constantinople seemed in danger of falling to the Muslims. In this context, Pseudo-Methodius's message would have been reassuring, at least as far as the immediate battle with Islam was concerned. Indeed, the battle for Constantinople had been long foretold, and the Christians would in fact prevail. This conflict would result in the accession of a Christian king in the Holy Land, and more important, all the key battles of the war would be fought in and around Jerusalem. The victory of Christianity over Islam would also signal the beginning of the final acts of history—a message that would have struck readers at the time of the crusade as startlingly relevant.

In the eleventh century, however, the specific conditions that had inspired Pseudo-Methodius to write his treatise no longer applied. After a century of rapid Muslim advance, the borders between the Islamic and Byzantine worlds had stabilized. In the tenth century, moreover, the Islamic empire had fragmented. The caliphate of Córdoba was founded in Spain in 929. The Middle East and North Africa, meanwhile, were divided between the Sunni Abbasid Caliphate, based in Baghdad, and the Shia Fatimid Caliphate, based in Cairo. The hostility between the adherents of the Sunni and Shia creeds is traditionally traced to a disagreement over the line of succession to the caliphate after the death of the Prophet in 632 CE. In the tenth century, Shia Islam gained a geographic and political base for the faith when the Fatimids—named after Fatima, the daughter of Muhammad—founded an independent state in Tunisia. Over the next half-century, Fatimid rule expanded throughout North Africa and into Syria and Palestine, where in 972 they seized control of Jerusalem. These momentous events received little mention in Europe. From the perspective of the rare Christian pilgrim to the Holy Land, the difference between one Muslim lord and another would have been negligible.

The situation changed under the sixth Fatimid caliph, al-Hakim bi Amr al-Lah (996–1021), who made a decision so momentous that it caused even Christians as far away as France to pay attention. For reasons still not clear, in 1004 al-Hakim initiated a broad persecution of Christians and Jews in his territory. As part of this initiative, he ordered the destruction of many churches, including the Church of the Holy Sepulcher in 1009. The magnitude of this event's impact on the Western world remains a point of historical controversy. In a letter attributed to Pope Sergius IV (r. 1009–1012), the writer condemns the caliph and calls upon Christians to retaliate. The letter's authenticity is uncertain. At least two contemporary French chroniclers heard about the desecration of Christ's tomb. One of them (see Document 10), surprisingly, blamed French Jews for the church's demolition. So inflammatory was the accusation that it set off the first major Jewish pogrom in the history of medieval Europe. Muslim sources, by contrast, argued that al-Hakim ordered the destruction of the Holy Sepulcher because he had learned that Christians were faking a miracle there every year—the famous ritual of the Holy Fire, in which the lamps in the church miraculously lit themselves on the day before Easter (see Document 11).

In 1028, with the cooperation of the new Fatimid caliph Ali az-Zahir, the Byzantine Empire began rebuilding the church. The end result was a basilica much smaller than the Constantinian original, but it was impressive enough that few of the crusaders seemed aware that it had ever been damaged. For the first time in history, however, great Christian edifices of the Holy Land had become flash points for religious conflict.

The Middle East grew still more chaotic with the advent of the Seljuk Turks, a tribal group from central Asia who in 1055 established themselves as effective rulers of Baghdad. The Abbasid caliphs remained the theoretical leaders of Sunni Islam, but the Seljuk sultans were in practice the real powers behind the caliphate. Renowned warriors, justly famous for their skills in archery and horsemanship, the Seljuks also began a new policy of military expansion, encroaching on both Fatimid and Byzantine lands and thus making the pilgrim's road to Jerusalem more dangerous.

Largely in ignorance of these political and cultural transformations, one of the largest groups of European pilgrims ever to travel to Jerusalem departed from Germany in 1064, with many of the participants believing that the end of the world would occur on Easter 1065 (see Documents 12 and 13). As they neared Jerusalem in March, they found themselves caught up in the midst of the Seljuk-Fatimid wars. Lacking the necessary conceptual vocabulary to interpret these events, the pilgrims who survived this journey fell back on what they thought they knew about Islam and in the process spread anxiety among their friends and fellow Christians about what was happening in Jerusalem and at the tomb of their savior.

As for the Turks, they continued their relentless expansion. Under the leadership of Alp Arslan, they won a major victory over the Byzantines at the Battle of Manzikert in 1071, moving their sphere of authority dangerously close to Constantinople. Two years later, Turkish armies seized control of Jerusalem, too, and returned it to Sunni practice. The new era of Seljuk rule, combined with the general instability in the region, further increased the danger for Christian pilgrims. The most frequent complaint that European travelers raised about the Turks, however, concerned money. The Turks, it seemed, were now charging unprecedented, punitively high taxes to Christians visiting Jerusalem, and they could be quite brutal when enforcing them.

But Europe itself was under no direct threat from Muslims in the Middle East. Byzantine Christians, however, were increasingly in danger due to the Seljuk expansion, but it is unlikely that many Western Christians knew or cared about their plight. Rumors were being whispered in the West—about wars waged by demonic armies, about atrocities committed against Christians, and above all about threats to the survival of the Holy Sepulcher, the birthplace of their religion and the city where the last acts of history would occur. Not a war for territory or for power in the conventional sense, the First Crusade was instead the product of this spiritual anxiety, a sense of prophetic mission born out of competing claims for the same small piece of sacred ground—territory that European Christians had previously been content to think of chiefly in terms of allegory and to visit only through stories, paintings, and sculpture (see Document 14).

THE CALL TO CRUSADE

In November 1095, Pope Urban II gave purpose and focus to this spiritual anxiety and excitement. His message combined the religious ideals embodied in Jerusalem with a doctrine of holy war that had, for two centuries, been dormant in both the East and the West. His reasons for doing so were various. In 1095, the papacy was entering into its twentieth year of warfare against the German emperor Henry IV and the rival pope, Clement III, usually called by historians "the antipope," whom Henry had appointed to serve his interests. Urban II had only recently, albeit temporarily, been able to reenter Rome after he and his predecessors had spent a decade in exile. Perhaps intending to press his advantage, Urban could have seen the crusade as a grand gesture that would unite the Latin Christian world. He had received a nudge in this direction from the Byzantine emperor Alexius I Comnenus, who was facing steady pressure on his eastern frontier from the Seljuk Turks. In March 1095, Alexius sent a delegation to a church council at Piacenza, where he made a direct appeal for the pope's help. The emperor also sought military assistance from at least one secular leader, Count Robert of Flanders. There followed eight months of careful consideration and consultation with bishops and counts until, on November 27, 1095, at the French city of Clermont (see the map on page 11), the pope revealed his bold plan to liberate Jerusalem in a sermon preached before a huge audience of clerics and laymen.

Unfortunately, we know very little about what Urban II actually said. Some historians have wondered if the pope mentioned Jerusalem at all, but the surviving record overwhelmingly indicates that he did. Most notable among the evidence is the famous "crusader indulgence," one of the few authentic sentences from Clermont to survive, recorded by Bishop Lambert of Arras, who was present at the council (see Document 15). In that statement, the pope promises that any soldier who sought to liberate Jerusalem would receive spiritual rewards. He does not offer forgiveness of sins. Rather, he promises remission of the penances for sins to which the soldiers had already confessed. Moreover, to receive even this narrowly defined indulgence, warriors needed to engage in combat with the right motives. The indulgence was thus subject to many restrictions and, as a result, surprisingly limited in scope.

Alongside this carefully worded indulgence we should also place a handful of more imaginative versions of what Urban II preached. None of these accounts—even two of them written by eyewitnesses—pretends to reveal the pope's actual words. Rather, they demonstrate what the individual historian felt, in retrospect, the pope ought to have preached. One of these writers, Robert the Monk, who actually attended the Council of Clermont, gives us numerous justifications for the crusade, ranging from cultural to spiritual to economic (see Document 16). He also focuses on the alleged crimes of Muslims, revealing in the process much of what Latin Christians knew, or thought they knew, about Islam. Another contemporary historian, Guibert of Nogent, who did not attend the council, repeats many of these same themes but integrates into them a sophisticated message, one that draws upon the ideas of Pseudo-Methodius (see Document 17). Neither of these historians is strictly accurate in the modern sense, but each of them reveals what

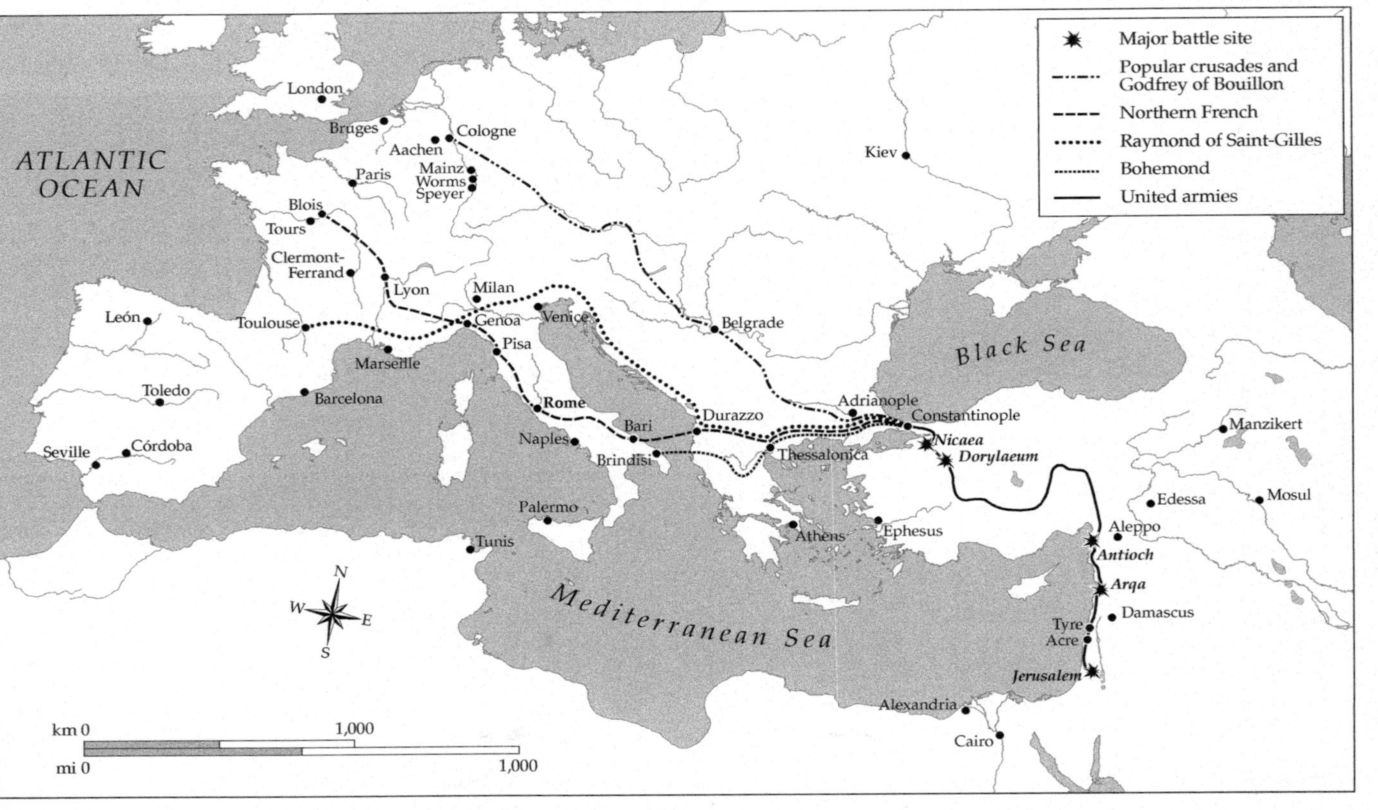

The Routes and Major Sites of the First Crusade

This map indicates the major landmarks of the First Crusade, as well as the sites at which major battles occurred. By tracing the various routes that different crusading groups took, from their origins north and west to their ultimate destination, Jerusalem, we can observe the points at which these armies crossed paths, diverged, and finally united.

contemporaries believed the crusade had in fact been about and also what kind of sermon they thought would have been most likely to appeal to Europe's warrior classes.

In framing their accounts of Urban II's sermon, these historians likely drew upon the message of less respectable, unlicensed preachers who were at the same time proclaiming the need for a crusade. Both Robert and Guibert, for example, had heard the most famous of the "popular" crusade preachers, Peter the Hermit. Neither of them thought much of him—each describes Peter as a hypocrite and rabble-rousing charlatan—but they also recognized his power and charisma. Other historians took an entirely more favorable view of the hermit. The German writer Albert of Aachen, who likely heard Peter preach, credits him with having invented the entire crusader movement (see Document 18). Based on another report, Peter seems to have derived his influence from a style of life based on the Gospel and from a message that was deeply apocalyptic (see Document 19). Traveling through France and Germany with a large entourage, he dressed in ragged clothes and avoided rich foods. The money he collected he applied toward charitable purposes, including the redemption of prostitutes. He rode on a mule, and his enthusiastic followers would pluck hairs from it, treating them as holy relics. In his sermons, he let listeners know that the end-time was near and that epic battles were soon to be fought in Jerusalem. By the spring of 1096, his followers included not only impoverished religious enthusiasts but also soldiers and nobles, all of them pledged to liberate Jerusalem from the unbelievers who held it—in their eyes—unjustly.

Inspired by the preaching of Urban II and men like Peter, princes, warriors, clerics, and ordinary men and women all across Europe began to take the cross—literally. Most had crosses sewn onto their garments. Some had them tattooed onto their bodies. The first prince known to have taken the cross is Count Raymond of Saint-Gilles, who had met with Urban II before the council of Clermont and had agreed to lend his support. Raymond probably expected to be named the armies' leader. One of the bishops in Raymond's territories, Adhémar of Le Puy, publicly agreed at Clermont to join the campaign and to act as the pope's special envoy, or legate, in the East. A handful of other leaders followed Raymond and Adhémar's examples. Notable among them were Hugh the Great, Count of Vermandois and brother of King Philip of France; Count Stephen of Blois and Chartres; Duke Robert of Normandy, son of William the Conqueror; Count Robert of Flanders, whom Emperor Alexius had helped recruit; and Duke Godfrey of Bouillon, leader of a Germanic contingent of crusaders. A mixture of personal piety, spiritual enthusiasm, and careful political calculation inspired all these men. But whatever the advantages, going on crusade was a risky and expensive endeavor. Not only would each of the princes have to provide for himself and his retinue during the journey, but his absence would leave his family and his property unprotected for an indefinite period. A crusader thus risked his life, social status, and all his possessions when he took the cross.

For one crusading contingent, however, the potential rewards of the campaign may have outweighed the risks. This was an army of Normans based in southern Italy. During the previous half-century, their families had arrived there as soldiers for hire, fighting against various enemies, including Muslims, Greeks, and even the pope. By the time of the crusade, due in large part to the leadership of a man named Robert Guiscard (ca. 1015–1085), they had established principalities of their own in Apulia, Calabria, and Sicily. In 1058, for reasons of marriage and politics, Robert Guiscard disinherited his firstborn son, a preternaturally large man called Bohemond. A leader of great ambitions but limited means, Bohemond heard the call to crusade while fighting for his uncle at Amalfi (see Document 20). He instantly recognized it as an opportunity—whether of a more political or spiritual character is uncertain—and quickly abandoned his uncle's retinue for Jerusalem, taking many of his fellow mercenaries with him.

Among them was Bohemond's nephew Tancred (see Document 21). A priest named Ralph of Caen, Tancred's biographer (Ralph himself settled in the Holy Land in 1107 and knew Tancred personally), gives a fascinating psychological portrait of what drove his hero to join the expedition. Tancred was, according to Ralph, genuinely worried about sins he had committed in battle. It was impossible, he believed, for a warrior to attain salvation. The crusade, however, provided a solution both elegant and miraculous—the chance to remain a soldier while earning forgiveness for sins. Other warriors, in the course of making their preparations for the journey east, committed similar ideas to writing. To defray the costs, they mortgaged all or some of their family property to wealthy, nearby churches. The monks at these churches would draw up special legal documents called "charters" to record these transactions. The charters specified that the donor of the land was going to Jerusalem for the sake of his soul, employing language very similar to what Ralph of Caen used regarding Tancred. The fear of sin was undoubtedly an important component of the crusader's psychology—though we can never be certain if it shows us what the warriors actually felt or what their monastic patrons wanted them to feel.

Our narrative sources cast light onto other aspects of the crusading mind-set, including an enthusiasm for the liberation of Jerusalem that borders on madness (see Document 22). One of the more troubling expressions of this radical spirituality was the treatment of the Jews by the first great wave of crusaders (see Document 23). Christian and Jewish accounts of the pogroms tell roughly the same story: The crusaders attacked the Jews out of a mixture of hatred, avarice, and religious zealotry. It is perhaps easy for modern readers to minimize that last point (piety) in favor of the first two (bigotry and greed), but in doing so we risk losing sight of perhaps the most surprising and disturbing aspect of the story: that Christians genuinely expected Jews to convert and that regardless of the coercion involved, they thought these conversions would be genuine. A few months later, the German emperor Henry IV (the same emperor with whom the papacy was at war) allowed the survivors of the pogroms to renounce Christianity and return to Judaism, a decision met with widespread disbelief and disappointment. This is one of the most difficult aspects of the crusade for modern readers to grasp. Anti-Jewish pogroms were, in the crusaders' eyes, an expression of genuine religiosity—a religiosity rooted in militant piety born of the spiritual and prophetic passions associated with the city of Jerusalem.

THE CRUSADE AND CONSTANTINOPLE

The armies inspired by Peter the Hermit were the first to leave their homelands. Most of them didn't make it past Hungary. In December 1096, however, several thousand of them reached Constantinople (see the map on page 11). Emperor Alexius must have been both disappointed and dumbstruck upon seeing them. He had written to Europe in hopes of attracting an army of well-trained mercenaries. What he got instead was a mixture of real warriors and poor pilgrims, most of them religious zealots like their shabbily dressed leader. Alexius would have known that other, better-organized armies were en route, but in the meantime he had to find a way to take care of this first, seemingly useless wave of pilgrims. We are fortunate to have a description of these events written by Anna Comnena, Alexius's daughter (see Document 24). Barely a teenager when the crusaders passed through Constantinople, she nonetheless understood and remembered enough to convey a uniquely Byzantine sensibility toward the Latin Christians. In brief, they struck her as barely civilized barbarians.

The cultural antagonisms in some ways only intensified when the main armies arrived, due in large part to the presence of Bohemond, who as a young man had led several military campaigns against Alexius (see the map on page 11). For this reason, Bohemond moved with extreme caution through Greek lands (see Document 25). Upon his arrival at Constantinople, he let Alexius know that he was more than willing to forget past unpleasantness and even to serve as the emperor's proxy among the crusade's leaders. Unlike the other Frankish princes, Bohemond knew how to speak the Byzantine language, literally and figuratively—an important skill, given the elevated and splendid character of Greek court life (see Document 26). Anna Comnena, predictably, describes Bohemond's motives with a fair dose of skepticism and a good deal of condescension (see Document 27). In her view, Alexius was in complete control of the Latin Christians, skillfully manipulating them at every turn so as to take the best possible advantage of their presence in the East.

Despite these tensions, the next stage of the campaign went more or less as Alexius hoped. The last of the Franks, as most contemporaries called the crusaders, departed Constantinople in May 1097, all of them joining together to lay siege to the city of Nicaea, the capital of the Turkish sultanate of Rum (see the map on page 11). Six weeks later, on June 19, 1097, due to close military cooperation between the Greeks and Latins, Nicaea surrendered. Fearing that the Franks might sack the city, Nicaea's leaders surrendered directly to Alexius. Some of the crusaders were disappointed not to be able to loot and plunder, but lavish gifts from Alexius quieted most of their complaints. Based on a letter written by the crusading prince Stephen of Blois to his wife, Adele, the whole process seems to have gone remarkably smoothly (see Document 28).

After ten days of rest, the crusaders continued their march toward Jerusalem, accompanied by a small contingent of Byzantine soldiers and a Greek military adviser named Tetigus. The army's immediate destination was Antioch, another former Byzantine capital that had recently fallen under Turkish control (see the map on page 11). For reasons not entirely clear, as soon as this phase of the march began, the Frankish host split into halves, each group following a slightly different path. On July 1, 1097, the one under the leadership of Bohemond had the misfortune to march into an ambush led by Kilij Arslan, the former ruler of Nicaea (see Documents 29 and 30). The tactics that both the Turks and Franks employed in this battle would set a pattern for the rest of the campaign. In brief, the Turks attempted to use their cavalry to encircle the Franks, all the while raining down arrows upon them. The Franks tried in every way to slow the Turks' cavalry maneuvers and to engage them at close quarters, where the heavier European armor and weaponry might provide them with a crucial advantage.

Despite the Turks' numerical advantage, the Franks' armor, weaponry, and battlefield tactics won the day. But the crusaders did not credit their victory to tactics and strategy alone. Some of them claimed to have seen saints joining the fray, bringing the wrath of heaven down upon their adversaries. After the battle, the Byzantine concept of the crusade—as a war of reconquest of former Greek lands—may have continued to hold some sway among the leaders. Many of the ordinary soldiers, however, were adopting the outlook of Peter the Hermit (who, it is prudent to remember, accompanied them all the way to Jerusalem). The crusade was primarily not a war about Eastern politics or even about the control of an earthly city. It was a campaign of such significance that God and his saints took an active part in its battles, the destiny of heaven seemingly intertwined with the fate of the Frankish host (see Document 31).

ANTIOCH: WHERE THE CRUSADE BECAME A HOLY WAR

When the crusaders reached Antioch on October 20, 1097, their numbers were greatly diminished. In addition to deaths from battle, disease, and starvation, they had been steadily garrisoning the towns they had formed alliances with or had conquered during the march. Additionally, Godfrey of Bouillon's brother Baldwin had abandoned the army, taking with him a contingent of warriors and heading into Syria, where he would soon establish himself as prince of Edessa.

To the soldiers who remained, Antioch offered a formidable challenge. Built onto a mountain slope, enclosed by high walls, partly hemmed in by the Orontes River, and fortified with hundreds of towers and a single massive citadel, the city was impossible to encircle; unlike Nicaea, the Franks could never completely cut it off from the outside world. They therefore built up what siege works they could manage, including three wooden towers and one bridge over the Orontes. All the while, they kept on guard against spies and possible raids from Antioch. On two occasions, they barely survived attacks from relief forces sent first from Damascus and then from Aleppo. Hunger and an unexpectedly harsh winter also proved deadly. It was all too much for Alexius's envoy Tetigus, who abandoned the siege in February, promising to return with reinforcements from Constantinople. But he was never seen again by the crusaders.

Against all probability, however, by March 1098 the Franks had survived the winter, had prevailed on the field several times against Antioch and its allies, and had even begun effectively to tighten their siege of the city (see Document 32). Sometime in April, the governor of Antioch, Yaghi-Siyan, opened negotiations with the Franks, and for a brief time in May the two sides agreed to a truce. This unexpected period of détente ended violently around May 20 when a group of Turks ambushed an unsuspecting party of Franks. The attack was probably the result of a deliberate decision by Yaghi-Siyan to end the truce. Word had reached the city that a massive relief force organized by Kerbogah, leader of Mosul, was approaching. In all likelihood, the crusade would be crushed between the walls of Antioch and this new army by early June.

At this point, Bohemond made a surprise announcement. At some time, perhaps during the truce, he had formed a friendship with a Turk named Pirrus, one of the city's defenders. Pirrus, it seemed, was willing to let the Franks enter Antioch at night through one of the towers he guarded. Bohemond, in exchange for having secured this act of treachery, asked the other lords to give him control of Antioch once they had captured it. At first reluctant, the Frankish princes—with the exception of Raymond of Saint-Gilles—agreed to the proposal, as otherwise their situation was hopeless. On June 3, 1098, Bohemond's plan went more or less as expected. Many sources, both Christian and Muslim (see Documents 33 and 34), describe the event, disagreeing on certain details but agreeing that the battle was something more akin to a slaughter. The Franks killed almost everyone they encountered—women, children, and any man with a beard. (Both Turks and Eastern Christians wore distinctive beards, but just to be on the safe side, Bishop Adhémar had ordered all the crusaders to shave so that they might be better able to distinguish friend from foe.) The only survivors were the Antiochenes, who had managed to hide during the sacking of the city, revealing themselves only when cooler heads prevailed. It was, effectively, the first occasion when the crusaders applied to combat the rules of holy war set down in Deuteronomy 20 (see Document 1).

But the Franks had no time to celebrate. Kerbogah, at the head of a massive relief force, arrived barely a day too late to save Antioch. Instead, he set up his own siege camps around the city, turning the crusaders' prize into a prison (see Document 35). The Franks' situation was now far worse than the Turks' had been over the previous eight months. Because of the long siege, Antioch's supplies were badly depleted. The Franks had also failed to capture the citadel, whose defenders could now conduct raids against the crusaders inside the city walls almost at will. And Kerbogah's army was far larger than the Franks' had been. When Stephen of Blois heard about the arrival of the relief force, he abandoned Syria altogether and headed back toward Constantinople. On the way, he reportedly informed Alexius that there was no need to try to save the Franks, for Kerbogah had already killed them all.

The crusaders inside Antioch could only hope for a miracle, putting their trust in prophecy, the intervention of saints (see Document 36), and, most famously, a fabulous military relic, the Holy Lance of Longinus, which had pierced Christ's side during his crucifixion (see Document 37). These supernatural factors do not explain how the Franks prevailed, but they were nonetheless essential to the army's survival. By this point, the soldiers were all learning to accept their identity as spiritual warriors. A key piece of evidence for this transformation can be found in their choice of a diplomatic emissary to send to Kerbogah on the eve of the final battle. The leaders selected as their spokesman not Adhémar of Le Puy or one of the other prominent and respected commanders. Instead, they sent Peter the Hermit, the original apocalyptic visionary, to make a last-ditch attempt to reason with their most fearsome enemy (see Document 38).

Peter's mission failed, leading to the crusaders' final confrontation with Kerbogah, on June 28, 1098. On that day, they adopted the one tactic that the Turks never foresaw. They abandoned the safety of Antioch's walls and took the fight directly to the enemy. It was an audacious, if not foolhardy, decision, a near-complete gamble for a miraculous victory through a surprise attack—and all of the writers who describe the battle do so in near-apocalyptic terms, none more so than one of the eyewitnesses, the priest Raymond of Aguilers. Raymond himself carried the Holy Lance into battle, waving it against the Turks as if it were a talisman (see Document 39). Through perfect faith, instruments of divine power, and the active intervention of saints, the crusaders won—or at least that is the position that all of the contemporary observers profess. Arab writers sought a different explanation for Kerbogah's loss, ascribing it not to religion but to treachery (see Document 40). Specifically, Kerbogah's own generals, chafing at his overbearing attitude, abandoned him at a crucial moment. There is likely some truth to this version of events. Yet as far as the Frankish rank and file were concerned, they had won an impossible victory, and they had done so through the miraculous power of God. The path to Jerusalem now lay open to them.

After Kerbogah's defeat, however, most of the Christian warriors were simply too exhausted to continue. Many of the knights and all of the princes wished to enjoy the fruits of their victory, to recover their strength, and to acquire a few more recruits before continuing with the expedition. The army also lost its most respected leader, Bishop Adhémar, who died of natural causes on August 1. Hugh the Great was sent to Constantinople to renew the Franks' pleas for help (to no avail, and Hugh never returned). The German leader Godfrey of Bouillon joined his brother at Edessa. Bohemond consolidated his hold on Antioch, but like Stephen and Hugh, he would soon abandon the crusade. After the trauma and deprivation and slaughter of Antioch, the armies needed months of rest before they could go on.

But not everyone was happy with this practical approach. This war, many of the Franks now believed, transcended the ordinary laws of combat. These fervent pilgrims pushed for an immediate march on Jerusalem, and they adopted as their rallying point the Holy Lance of Antioch, the relic that had delivered them from their most recent nightmare. They also found a willing spokesman for their cause in the person of Peter Bartholomew, a poor and near illiterate pilgrim whose visions had led to the lance's discovery. Because of the close association of this relic with Count Raymond of Saint-Gilles, the lance also became a symbol of pride among his Provençal followers rather than a universal sign of the crusade's shared victory over Kerbogah, thus further exacerbating divisions in the army.

By the time the Franks had reached the Syrian city of Arqa (see the map on page 11), northern European soldiers were openly questioning the validity of the Holy Lance, suggesting that it was an elaborate Provençal hoax. Under mounting pressure from all sides, Peter Bartholomew offered to undergo a spectacular ordeal by fire on April 8, 1099. If Peter survived, the army would recognize the lance as genuine. If he did not, the Franks would, with difficulty, admit that this great symbol of victory was a fraud. Unfortunately for both sides, the issue would remain in doubt. Peter survived his trial by fire, but only for twelve days, leaving the result open to dispute. Did his twelve-day survival mean that the Holy Lance was truly the weapon that had pierced Christ's side, or did his eventual death mean it was a hoax?

The army remained divided into factions, and relations between the Provençals and everyone else grew hopelessly poisoned (see Document 41). Raymond of Saint-Gilles, who had been benefiting from his role as patron of the lance, now found his military authority undermined. Just a few days' march from Jerusalem, the crusade was on the verge of collapse, torn apart by its own spiritual fervor and by the divisive visions of one of its own prophets.

JERUSALEM: THE BATTLE FOR HEAVEN

At about the same time as Peter Bartholomew's trial, the Franks finally received a delegation from Alexius, telling them that he was going to join them in midsummer. In principle, this was good news. In practice, given Alexius's desire to reclaim Antioch and his possible interest in restoring Jerusalem to Greek rule, his arrival had the potential to scuttle the crusade. More pressingly, the Franks also learned of other surprising developments: Jerusalem had been conquered. Armies from the Fatimid Caliphate had driven the Seljuk Turks out of the city and restored it to Egyptian control. If the Fatimids properly garrisoned the city, it would be impossible for the surviving remnant of the crusading host to capture it; by this point, the original force of up to 100,000 men had probably declined to somewhere near 10,000.

Recognizing how dire their situation had become, most of the princes decided to push forward. Raymond of Aguilers alone wanted to stay in Arqa, probably to claim the city for himself and to use it as a base from which to harass Bohemond at Antioch. He gave up on this dream only after his followers set their own tents on fire. Finally, on May 13, 1099, the crusaders abandoned Arqa, but the divisions were not healed. The Provençals remained devoted to the Holy Lance and to the memory of Peter Bartholomew. The northern Europeans rallied around a golden cross sculpted by Arnulf of Chocques, chaplain to Robert of Normandy. Divided into clear factions, they reached Jerusalem on June 7 (see Documents 42, 43, and 44).

Perhaps the army's leaders were, at this point, a little too confident in their divine calling, for after less than a week, they ordered an attack on the city. This time there was no miracle. The assault failed, and the crusaders realized that they would have to prepare for a longer siege. But not too long—a Muslim relief force from Egypt was expected to arrive any day, and there was so little potable water near Jerusalem that all of the soldiers faced the very real possibility of dying of thirst. Simply put, trying to starve out the Muslim garrison was not an option. Instead, they would have to make a second attempt at storming the city, though this time with a better plan. In preparation, they established camps on opposite sides of the city—with the northern Europeans to the north and the Provençals to the south at Mount Zion. By establishing these two points of attack, the Franks could force the Egyptians to split their military resources. But the two camps also represented the ugly new reality of the campaign: The northerners and the Provençals were barely able to work together.

Before the final attack, the army made one last attempt to get its spiritual house in order. Together, both factions made a procession around the city on July 8 (see Document 45), deliberately calling to mind the Old Testament story of Joshua and the Battle of Jericho. The procession included speeches from the army's remaining spiritual leaders—Peter the Hermit, Arnulf of Chocques, and Raymond of Aguilers, among others. We know a little of what they said. The most riveting prebattle sermon reaches us not from an eyewitness but from a historian who never left Europe, Baudry of Bourgueil (see Document 46). Baudry put into the mouth of an unnamed preacher a gripping oration about the supernatural stakes of the battle. Not just a war for the earthly Jerusalem, it was also a conflict for the heavenly one, a distinction that was becoming increasingly difficult to make as the campaign approached its climax. How closely this message reflected actual battlefield orations, we can't be sure. We can say, however, that the sermon reflects Baudry's understanding, with just a few years' hindsight, of what the crusade had been about.

The assault began a week later, on July 14. The Provençals, attacking from Mount Zion, made very little progress. In the face of a ferocious catapult bombardment from inside the city, they could not maneuver their siege equipment close enough to provide any sort of cover for a ground attack. On the other side of Jerusalem, the northern Europeans used a massive battering ram to break through the first section of a double wall, but by the end of the day, they still had not managed to enter the city. When the fighting resumed on July 15, the Provençals' attack was on the verge of complete failure. The northerners, however, maneuvered a mobile wooden tower through the breach in the first city wall and managed to fashion a makeshift bridge between the top of the tower and the ramparts of the second wall. A few of the Franks staked out a position there, and the city's defenders gave way. Almost immediately, the battle turned into a massacre.

The pent-up frustrations and apocalyptic expectations of the previous three years burst forth. Warriors reported seeing saints, ghosts, and mysterious riders on white horses. One of the army's leaders later claimed to have come face-to-face with a statue of Antichrist hidden inside the Dome of the Rock. Eyewitnesses recalled blood flowing ankle-deep through the streets; Raymond of Aguilers, influenced by the book of Revelation, imagined the level of blood to be much higher. The Franks who witnessed the slaughter believed it unprecedented and a cause for celebration (see Documents 47 and 48). Arab historians felt a corresponding horror at these events, claiming the death toll to be as high as seventy thousand (see Document 49)—a clear exaggeration, though an indication of the imaginative impact, or perhaps the historical trauma, created in the Muslim world by the loss of Jerusalem.

The killing, however, did not end on July 15. Over the next two days, there occurred a systematic massacre of prisoners—men, women, and children—that must have caused some of the crusaders to feel real qualms about what they were doing (see Document 50). However brutal life may have been in eleventh-century Europe, this methodical application of the rules of holy war would have been far beyond the realm of any of the warriors' experiences. In the end, only a handful of Muslim and Jewish prisoners escaped with their lives, most of them ransomed by Raymond of Saint-Gilles from the Tower of David, the main citadel in Jerusalem. Those crusaders who had expected to find an apocalypse in Jerusalem created something very much like it through their own weapons and force of will. In any case, the battle left in the Latin historical imagination an indelible sense of the connections between crusaders, Christ, and prophetic expectations (see Document 51).

AFTERMATH

News of Jerusalem's capture was greeted in Europe with joy and astonishment. It was a reaction that ecclesiastical leaders deliberately cultivated. In a letter from Archbishop Manasses of Reims to Bishop Lambert of Arras, for example, Manasses ordered celebrations of the battle to be held in all the churches in his archdiocese (see Document 52). He also requested prayers for some of the fallen battle heroes, whom the archbishop considered martyrs. Other evidence of European reaction is scattered throughout this book, for the First Crusade inspired an unprecedented literary response. At least a dozen full-length prose narratives were composed to celebrate the victory at Jerusalem, not counting epic poems in Latin and in the vernacular. Through these texts and liturgical festivities, European Christians from all walks of life declared that their culture—a Latin, Christian culture—had established itself as an active player in the historical destiny of the world.

A concerted reaction in the Muslim world—a counter-crusade, as it were—was slow to develop. Reasons for this lack of response are various. Not only was there the obvious division between Sunni and Shia Muslims, but there also existed significant differences within those confessional groups. Often intra-Muslim and intra-Turkish feuds trumped any sense of religious loyalty. Indeed, one of the most surprising developments in the aftermath of the crusade was the tendency of Frankish and Turkish armies to form alliances with one another, occasionally against other Frankish-Turkish coalitions. The Franks of Jerusalem similarly learned to play the Fatimid Caliphate and the Abbasid Caliphate against each other. Survival in the political world of the Middle East did not allow the settled crusaders to maintain their original ideological purity.

The first Arab writer to call for a unified response to the crusade was a Damascene jurist named Ali ibn Tahir al-Sulami, in an 1105 treatise titled *Kitab al-Jihad*, or *Book of Holy War* (see Document 53). It was in many respects a visionary work. For the first time, an Arab writer described the crusaders in religious terms—men engaged in a jihad against Islam. Al-Sulami put this shocking development into a broad historical context. In the early years of Islam, Muslims had practiced jihad as an annual rite. Even if formal raids were not organized during the course of a year, individual communities would attack unbelievers on their own initiative. That practice, however, had fallen into disuse. As a result, Christians in Western lands sensed weakness in Islam and had begun waging an all-out campaign against it, first in Sicily, then in Spain, and now in Jerusalem. Al-Sulami thus imagined a far more unified campaign than did the crusaders themselves. The only feasible response to this Christian jihad was for Islam to answer in kind, to revive its dormant tradition of holy war. Ironically, in arguing for his program of renewed jihad, al-Sulami employed language strikingly similar to the Christian crusaders'.

Al-Sulami's message sounds compelling, but Muslim leaders did not embrace it for another half-century. They did so then due to the leadership of two famous generals, Nur ad-Din (1118–1174) and Saladin (1137–1193). In 1187, Saladin recaptured Jerusalem, but crusader settlements would endure in one form or another in the Middle East until 1291. Despite the fall of Jerusalem, the repercussions of crusading warfare continued to be felt throughout the medieval and into the early modern period. Recent jihadist language seeks to make the 9/11 attacks of 2001 and the ensuing War on Terror the latest chapter in the same saga. Any attempt to directly connect the eleventh century to the twenty-first is obviously misguided. Still, it is impossible not to hear faint echoes of medieval holy wars in modern political-religious rhetoric. That is the First Crusade's unfortunate legacy: a conception of holy warfare coupled with prophetic thought, built on profound cultural misunderstandings, which has survived centuries and still haunts modern sensibilities in both the East and the West.

NOTES

[1] Guibert of Nogent, *Dei gesta per Francos*, ed. R. B. C. Huygens, Corpus Christianorum Continuatio Mediaevalis 127A (Turnhout: Brepols, 1996), 87.

[2] Ibid., 125.

[3] Luke 3:14.

[4] The writer is usually called by historians Bartolph de Nangis, published as *Gesta Francorum Iherusalem expugnantium*, in Recueil des Historiens des Croisades, *Historiens occidentaux* 3 (Paris: Imprimerie Royale, 1866), 515.

[5] The legendary founder of Judaism was the patriarch Abraham, and the Jews believed themselves to be descendants of his second son, Isaac. Christianity, in its earliest incarnation, was a sect of Judaism. Arabs believed themselves descended from Abraham's first-born son, Ishmael.

[6] In Matthew 24:36, for example, Christ tells his apostles that not even the angels know the hour when history will end, but earlier in the same chapter he describes events that will precede the Last Days, concluding, "Even so, when you see all these things, you know that it is near, right at the door" (Matthew 24:33).

PART TWO

The Documents

1

Holy War

1

DEUTERONOMY 20

An Old Testament Theory of Holy War

The New Testament has no doctrine of holy war. Christian theologians would have had to turn instead to the Old Testament to discover any guidelines for how to fight in the name of God. The most important such passage appears in the book of Deuteronomy, believed to contain the laws pronounced by Moses on the eve of the Israelites' entrance into the Promised Land.[1]

1 Should you go to war against your enemies and see horsemen and chariots and an opposing army greater in number than yours, do not fear them, because the Lord your God, who brought you up out of Egypt, is with you. 2 As you approach them in battle, the priest will stand at the head of the army and address the people thus: 3 "Hear, Israel: Today you are taking the fight to your enemies. Let your heart not tremble; do not fear them; do not give ground to them and be not terrified by them. 4 For the Lord your God is in your midst and will fight on your side against your enemies, snatching you from every danger."

5 The dukes shall say to each division, so that the whole army might hear: "Has anyone built a new house and not yet lived in it? Let him go

[1] This translation is from the Vulgate Bible, the Latin translation of the Bible commonly used in medieval Europe. Although this version differs in significant ways from modern translations, I have based my translation on it because it is the one with which crusaders and their clerical counselors would have been most familiar.

Deuteronomy 20, translated from the Vulgate. Translated by the author.

and return to his home, lest he die in battle and someone else claim it.
6 Has anyone planted a vineyard and not distributed its fruits? Let him
go and return to his home, lest he die in battle and someone else obtain
those rights. 7 Is anyone now betrothed to a woman and not yet married to her? Let him go and return to his home, lest he die in battle and
another man take her." 8 These things said, they shall add the rest, saying, "Is anyone fearful or fainthearted? Let him go and return to home,
lest he make his brothers as fearful as he is." 9 When the army's dukes
have fallen silent and have made an end of speech, each one shall prepare his divisions to fight.

10 When you approach a city to attack it, first offer it peace. 11 If they
accept and open their gates to you, all the people in it shall be spared
and will be made your tributary slaves. 12 But if they refuse your offer of
peace and initiate battle against you, you will attack them. 13 And when
the Lord your God delivers that city into your hands, you will strike
down every one of the males there, putting them to the sword, 14 except-
ing the women, the children, the livestock, and other goods in the city.
These you may distribute as plunder to the troops, and you may eat
from the spoils of your enemies, which the Lord your God gives to you.
15 This is how you are to treat all the cities that are a great distance from
you and that you are not going to claim as a possession.

16 As for those cities that will be given into your possession, do not
allow anyone in them to live. 17 No! Kill them all at sword point—the
Hittites, Amorites, Canaanites, Perizzites, Hivites, and Jebusites[2]—thus
the Lord your God has commanded you. 18 Otherwise, they will teach
you to offer the abominations that they sacrifice to their gods, and you
will sin against the Lord your God.

19 When you besiege a city for a long time and when you surround
it with siege machines[3] to conquer it, do not cut down the trees whose
fruit you can eat. Do not put the surrounding lands to the ax. Are trees
people, able to raise a numerous army against you? 20 That said, you
may cut down trees that do not bear fruit and put them to appropriate use, building siege machines, until you capture the city that fought
against you.

[2] These are the tribes that occupied the Promised Land and were to be exterminated because of their practice of idol worship.

[3] Siege machines include all the heavy equipment of siege warfare. In the eleventh century, this would chiefly have meant mobile towers, battering rams, and catapults.

2

1 SAMUEL 15

Holy War in Action

In addition to guidelines for how to fight a holy war, the Old Testament contains stories that illustrate its practice. This selection describes a battle between the Israelites and the Amalekites, another of the tribal groups in Israel thought to be descended from Esau, the twin brother of the Jewish patriarch Jacob. This battle was fought shortly after the elevation of Saul as the first king of Israel.

1 And Samuel said to Saul, "The Lord sent me to anoint you king over his
people Israel; so listen now to the voice of the Lord. 2 The Lord of Hosts
says: 'I have recollected how the Amalekites blocked the Israelites'
path as they came up from Egypt. 3 Now go, strike Amalek and destroy
it completely. Do not spare them and do not wish for their goods; kill
every man and woman, each child and babe, cattle and sheep, camels
and asses.'" 4 Saul thus told these things to his people and herded them
together like sheep: two hundred thousand foot soldiers and ten thousand men from Judah. 5 And when Saul reached the city of Amalek, he
set an ambush in the ravine. 6 And he said to the Cenites,[1] "Go away,
depart, and leave the Amalekites lest I destroy you with them. You
showed mercy to all the sons of Israel when they came up out of Egypt."
And the Cenites withdrew from the Amalekites.

7 Then Saul attacked the Amalekites all the way from Havilah to Sur,
which is near Egypt. 8 And he captured Agag, king of the Amalekites,
alive, and all his people he killed at sword point. 9 But Saul and the
army spared Agag and saved the best of the sheep and cattle, their garments and their rams and whatever seemed desirable to them. These
they did not wish to destroy completely, but everything that seemed
vile and worthless they destroyed. 10 Then the word of the Lord came
to Samuel and said: 11 "I regret that I ever made Saul king, because he

[1] Yet another tribe inhabiting the Promised Land. Traditionally believed to have aided the Israelites during the Exodus, they are shown mercy here by Saul.

1 Samuel 15, translated from the Vulgate. Translated by the author.

has abandoned me and has not carried out my words." Samuel was saddened, and he cried out to the Lord all that night.

12 When night turned to morning, Samuel arose and went to meet Saul but was told that Saul had gone to Mount Carmel and there had raised a triumphal arch for himself and then had gone down to Gilgal. Samuel therefore went to Saul, and Saul was offering a sacrifice to the Lord taken from the first fruits of plunder he had claimed from Amalek. 13 When Samuel had come to him, Saul said, "The Lord bless you! I have fulfilled the word of God!" 14 But Samuel said, "What then is this bleating of sheep that rings in my ears or the lowing of cattle that I hear?" 15 And Saul said, "The army brought these things from Amalek; they spared the best of the sheep and cattle to sacrifice to the Lord your God; the rest we slaughtered."

16 Then Samuel said to Saul, "Let me tell you what the Lord said to me last night." And Saul said to him, "Speak." 17 And Samuel said, "Although once you were small in your own eyes, did you not become the head of the tribes of Israel? And did not the Lord anoint you king over Israel? 18 And did not the Lord set you on this path, saying, 'Go and kill the sinful Amalekites and fight against them until you have destroyed them'? 19 Why did you not listen to the voice of the Lord? Why did you turn to plunder and do evil in the eyes of the Lord?" 20 And Saul said to Samuel, "But I did listen to the voice of the Lord, and I walked the path on which the Lord set me. I brought back Agag, king of the Amalekites, and I killed the Amalekites. 21 The army took sheep and cattle for plunder to sacrifice it to the Lord God at Gilgal." 22 And Samuel said: "Does the Lord delight in sacrifices and offerings more than in having the voice of the Lord obeyed? Obedience is better than any sacrifice, and to listen is better than to offer the fat of rams. 23 For rebellion is like the sin of divination, and arrogance like the crime of idolatry. Because you have rejected the word of the Lord, the Lord has rejected you as king."

24 And Saul said to Samuel, "I have sinned, because I have turned away from the word of the Lord and from your instructions, out of fear of the army and in obedience to their wishes. 25 Now I beg you, forgive my sin and come back with me, so that I may worship the Lord." 26 And Samuel said to Saul, "I will not go back with you. You have rejected the word of the Lord, and the Lord has rejected you as king over Israel."

3

SURAH 8

Holy War in the Qur'an

This surah, or chapter, from the Qur'an contains guidelines for the proper practice of war in the Islamic world. Much of the surah, however, refers to a specific event: the Battle of Badr in 624, the first major engagement between Muhammad's armies from Medina and their enemies from Mecca. In addition to rules about plunder and its distribution, the text discusses the proper handling of oath breakers, the role of angels and evil spirits in battle, and how to treat prisoners.

9 When ye sought help of your Lord and He answered you (saying): I
will help you with a thousand of the angels, rank on rank.
10 Allah appointed it only as good tidings, and that your hearts
thereby might be at rest. Victory cometh only by the help of Allah. Lo!
Allah is Mighty, Wise.
11 When He made the slumber fall upon you as a reassurance from
him and sent down water from the sky upon you, that thereby He might
purify you, and remove from you the fear of Satan, and make strong
your hearts and firm (your) feet thereby.
12 When thy Lord inspired the angels, (saying): I am with you. So
make those who believe stand firm. I will throw fear into the hearts of
those who disbelieve. Then smite the necks and smite of them each
finger.
13 That is because they opposed Allah and His messenger. Whoso
opposeth Allah and His messenger, (for him) lo! Allah is severe in
punishment.
14 That (is the award), so taste it, and (know) that for disbelievers is
the torment of the Fire.
15 O ye who believe! When ye meet those who disbelieve in battle,
turn not your backs to them.

Surah 8, "The Spoils of War," in *The Meaning of the Glorious Koran*, trans. Marmaduke Pickthall (New York: Alfred A. Knopf, 1930), 139–44.

[16] Whoso on that day turneth his back to them, unless manoeuvring for battle or intent to join a company, he truly hath incurred wrath from Allah, and his habitation will be hell, a hapless journey's end.

[17] Ye (Muslims) slew them not, but Allah slew them. And thou (Muhammad) threwest not when thou didst throw, but Allah threw, that He might test the believers by a fair test from Him. Lo! Allah is Hearer, Knower.

. . .

[41] And know that whatever ye take as spoils of war, lo! a fifth thereof is for Allah, and for the messenger and for the kinsman (who hath need) and orphans and the needy and the wayfarer, if ye believe in Allah and that which We revealed unto Our slave on the Day of Discrimination,[1] the day when the two armies met. And Allah is Able to do all things.

[42] When ye were on the near bank (of the valley) and they were on the yonder bank, and the caravan was below you (on the coast plain). And had ye trysted to meet one another ye surely would have failed to keep the tryst, but (it happened, as it did, without the forethought of either of you) that Allah might conclude a thing that must be done; that he who perished (on that day) might perish by a clear proof (of His Sovereignty) and he who survived might survive by a clear proof (of His Sovereignty). Lo! Allah in truth is Hearer, Knower.

[43] When Allah showed them unto thee (O Muhammad) in thy dream as few in number, and if He had shown them to thee as many, ye (Muslims) would have faltered and would have quarrelled over the affair. But Allah saved (you). Lo! He knoweth what is in the breasts (of men).[2]

[44] And when He made you (Muslims), when ye met (them), see them with your eyes as few, and lessened you in their eyes, (it was) that Allah might conclude a thing that must be done. Unto Allah all things are brought back.

[45] O ye who believe! When ye meet an army, hold firm and think of Allah much, that ye may be successful.

[46] And obey Allah and His messenger, and dispute not one with another lest ye falter and your strength depart from you; but be steadfast! Lo! Allah is with the steadfast.

[1] Or "the day of testing," which is the day of the Battle of Badr, March 13, 624.

[2] God thus showed the Prophet in a dream that the enemy would be fewer than they actually were. Had God revealed the actual number of the enemy, Muhammad's armies might have been less willing to confront them.

47 Be not as those who came forth from their dwellings boastfully and to be seen of men, and debar (men) from the way of Allah, while Allah is surrounding all they do.

48 And when Satan[3] made their deeds seem fair to them and said: No-one of mankind can conquer you this day, for I am your protector. But when the armies came in sight of one another, he took flight, saying: Lo! I am guiltless of you. Lo! I see that which ye see not. Lo! I fear Allah. And Allah is severe in punishment.[4]

49 When the hypocrites and those in whose hearts is a disease said: Their religion hath deluded these. Whoso putteth his trust in Allah (will find that) lo! Allah is Mighty, Wise.

50 If thou couldst see how the angels receive those who disbelieve, smiting faces and their backs and (saying): Taste the punishment of burning!

51 This is for that which your own hands have sent before (to the Judgment), and (know) that Allah is not a tyrant to His slaves.

52 (Their way is) as the way of Pharaoh's folk and those before them;[5] they disbelieved the revelations of Allah, and Allah took them in their sins. Lo! Allah is Strong, severe in punishment.

53 That is because Allah never changeth the grace He hath bestowed on any people until they first change that which is in their hearts, and (that is) because Allah is Hearer, Knower.

54 (Their way is) as the way of Pharaoh's folk and those before them; they denied the revelations of their Lord, so We destroyed them in their sins. And We drowned the folk of Pharaoh. All were evil-doers.

55 Lo! the worst of beasts in Allah's sight are the ungrateful who will not believe;

56 Those of them with whom thou madest a treaty, and then at every opportunity they break their treaty, and they keep not duty (to Allah).

57 If thou comest on them in the war, deal with them so as to strike fear in those who are behind them, that haply they may remember.

58 And if thou fearest treachery from any folk, then throw back to them (their treaty) fairly. Lo! Allah loveth not the treacherous.

[3] Satan, or *Shaitan*, appears in Surah 7 of the Qur'an. An angel too proud to bow before Adam, the first man, he becomes a spirit who seeks to lead humanity astray until Judgment Day.

[4] The armies of the enemy thus fight under the influence of a malign spirit.

[5] A reference to the story of the Exodus, the Israelites' flight from Egypt. Muhammad's enemies refused to believe in divine warnings and suffered a fate similar (as noted in verse 54) to drowning in the Red Sea.

59 And let not those who disbelieve suppose that they can outstrip (Allah's Purpose). Lo! they cannot escape.

60 Make ready for them all thou canst of (armed) force and of horses tethered, that thereby ye may dismay the enemy of Allah and your enemy, and others beside them whom ye know not. Allah knoweth them. Whatsoever ye spend in the way of Allah it will be repaid to you in full, and ye will not be wronged.

61 And if they incline to peace, incline thou also to it, and trust in Allah. Lo! He, even He, is the Hearer, the Knower.

62 And if they would deceive thee, then lo! Allah is Sufficient for thee. He it is Who supporteth thee with His help and with the believers,

63 And (as for the believers) hath attuned their hearts. If thou hadst spent all that is in the earth thou couldst not have attuned their hearts, but Allah hath attuned them.[6] Lo! He is Mighty, Wise.

64 O Prophet! Allah is Sufficient for thee and those who follow thee of the believers.

65 O Prophet! Exhort the believers to fight. If there be of you twenty steadfast they shall overcome two hundred, and if there be of you a hundred (steadfast) they shall overcome a thousand of those who disbelieve, because they (the disbelievers) are a folk without intelligence.

66 Now hath Allah lightened your burden, for He knoweth that there is weakness in you. So if there be of you a steadfast hundred they shall overcome two hundred, and if there be of you a thousand (steadfast) they shall overcome two thousand by permission of Allah. Allah is with the steadfast.

67 It is not for any prophet to have captives until he hath made slaughter in the land. Ye desire the lure of this world and Allah desireth (for you) the Hereafter, and Allah is Mighty, Wise.

68 Had it not been for an ordinance of Allah which had gone before, an awful doom had come upon you on account of what ye took.

69 Now enjoy what ye have won, as lawful and good, and keep your duty to Allah. Lo! Allah is Forgiving, Merciful.[7]

70 O Prophet! Say unto those captives who are in your hands: If Allah knoweth any good in your hearts He will give you better than that which hath been taken from you, and will forgive you. Lo! Allah is Forgiving, Merciful.

[6] That is, Allah has created unity of purpose among the soldiers.

[7] Verses 67–69 refer to prisoners taken after the Battle of Badr. The decision to spare prisoners was apparently controversial, justified here by an appeal to divine authority.

71 And if they would betray thee, they betrayed Allah before, and He gave (thee) power over them. Allah is Knower, Wise.

72 Lo! those who believed and left their homes and strove with their wealth and their lives for the cause of Allah, and those who took them in and helped them: these are protecting friends one of another. And those who believed but did not leave their homes, ye have no duty to protect them till they leave their homes; but if they seek help from you in the matter of religion then it is your duty to help (them) except against a folk between whom and you there is a treaty. Allah is Seer of what ye do.

2

Jerusalem

4

IBN ISHAQ

Jerusalem in Islamic Tradition: The Night Journey of Muhammad

Eighth Century

Over a hundred years after the death of Muhammad, the Muslim historian Ibn Ishaq, working mainly with oral traditions, assembled a massive biography of the prophet, called the Sirat Rasul Allah, *or* Life of the Messenger of God. *These excerpts from that work give a brief, early account of the Mi'raj, the prophet's ascent from Jerusalem into heaven. The excerpts indicate the oral character of the traditional stories of the Mi'raj while illustrating concretely the mystical and historical significance of Jerusalem for Muslims.*

Abdullah ibn Masud used to tell (as others have reported to me) the following: "Buraq, the steed whom all the other prophets had ridden and whose hooves with each stride reached as far as the eye could see, was led to Muhammad, and his friend Gabriel helped him onto it and guided him around the wonders of heaven and earth, until he eventually reached Jerusalem. Here he found Abraham, Moses, Jesus, and other

Mohammed Ibn Ishak, *Das Leben Mohammed's*, ed. Abd el-Malik Ibn Hischam, trans. Gustav Weil, 2 vols. (Stuttgart: J. B. Metzler'schen, 1864). This translation by the author is based on Weil's German translation.

prophets, who had gathered together to meet him, and they prayed with him. Three vessels were then brought to him—one containing milk, another wine, and a third water. As these vessels were set before him, Muhammad heard a voice call: 'If he takes the water, he and his people will drown. If he takes the wine, he and his people will fall into error. But if he takes the milk, he and his people will be rightly guided.' Muhammad himself said, 'Therefore I took the vessel with the milk and drank from it, and Gabriel said to me, "You will be rightly guided and your people with you, o Muhammad!"'"

Al-Hasan told me that Muhammad himself said, "While I was sleeping in the sanctuary,[1] Gabriel came and jostled me with his foot. I sat upright, but saw nothing and lay down again in the same place. Once again he jostled me with his foot. I got up, but saw nothing and lay down again. A third time he jostled me, and as I sat upright, he took me by the arm. When I stood, he led me to the sanctuary's door. A white animal was standing, its form somewhere between a mule and ass, with two wings on its sides and with forelegs that reached as far as the eye could see. Gabriel raised me onto it and led me forward and stayed by my side."

Qatada reported to me that Muhammad told him: "When I approached the animal to mount him, Gabriel placed a hand on its mane to steady it, and he said, 'Are you not ashamed, Buraq? By God, you have never been mounted by a servant of God nobler than Muhammad!' Buraq was so ashamed that he became covered in sweat, and then he stood still so that I might mount him."

Al-Hasan reported, "Muhammad went forth then, led on by Gabriel, to Jerusalem, where he found Abraham, Moses, Jesus, and other Prophets. Muhammad led them in prayer, and then two vessels were brought to him. In one of them was wine, and in the other, milk. Muhammad took the vessel with milk and drank from it and left the wine alone. Then Gabriel said to him, 'You have been rightly guided through creation, as will your people; and wine shall be forbidden to you.' Then Muhammad returned to Mecca, and the next morning he told what had happened to the Quraysh.[2] Most of the people said, 'Oh, that makes perfect sense!

[1] The Ka'ba, the cube-shaped building in Mecca that is venerated as the most sacred location in the Islamic world. The *qibla*, or direction to face during prayer, is provided by the Ka'ba.

[2] The dominant tribe in Mecca, most of whose clan leaders opposed the preaching of Muhammad.

Muhammad can in one night make the trip to Syria, there and back again, when a caravan needs two months to do the same thing!' . . ."

. . .

A trustworthy man has told me that he heard from Abu Sa'id al Khudri that he had heard Muhammad say, "When I had finished my work in Jerusalem, a ladder was brought to me lovelier than anything I had ever seen. It is the ladder to which the dying man will direct his gaze at the resurrection. My friend Gabriel permitted me to climb it until we had come to one of the gates of heaven, the one called 'Gate of the Watchmen.' There stood an angel called Isma'il, who had over twelve thousand angels under his command, each of whom had another twelve thousand angels under his command." While telling this story, Muhammad would say, "Only he knows the armies of your lord."[3] "As I came before the door, Isma'il asked, 'Who is this man, Gabriel?' Gabriel answered, 'It is Muhammad.' Isma'il then asked, 'Has he already been chosen as a prophet?' Gabriel answered: 'Yes.' Then he said, 'Good,' and he wished me luck.'"

[3] Surah 74:34.

5

A View of Jerusalem from the Mount of Olives

In the foreground of the image here is the Temple Mount, with al-Aqsa Mosque to the left and the Dome of the Rock toward the center. The city walls were built in the sixteenth century, but they closely follow the path of the walls as they stood at the time of the First Crusade.

6

NAṢER-E KHOSRAW

A Muslim Pilgrim's Description of Jerusalem

ca. 1046–1052

The Muslim writer Naṣer-e Khosraw (1004–1088) experienced a dream vision that inspired him to temporarily abandon a lucrative administrative position in the Islamic capital of Khorasan, in modern Iran, in order to undertake the hajj, the pilgrimage to Mecca. His journey, which he describes in detail, lasted from 1046 to 1052. One of the places he visited was Jerusalem, and his description of the Haram al-Sharif (or Temple Mount) provides a clear and concise explanation for how and why Muslims at the time of the First Crusade venerated Jerusalem as much as Latin Christians did.

The hospital and Friday mosque are on the eastern side of the city, and one wall of the mosque is on the Valley of Gehenna. Looking at the wall from outside the mosque, one can see that it is one hundred cubits[1] high and made of large, unmortared stones. Inside the mosque [area] the top of the wall is level. The mosque was built in that place because it is the site of the very rock which God commanded Moses to make the direction of prayer. When this commandment came, Moses did make it the direction of prayer; not long thereafter he died. Then, in the time of Solomon, as the rock was still the direction of prayer, the mosque was built around the rock, with the rock in the middle. This rock remained the direction people faced for prayer until the time of the Prophet Mohammad, when God commanded the direction to be toward the Ka'ba [in Mecca]. . . .

In the south corner of the east wall is an underground mosque, to reach which you must descend many steps. It is twenty by fifteen ells[2]

[1] An ancient unit of measurement, usually estimated at around eighteen inches.

[2] Another archaic unit of measurement, roughly the length from the hand to the elbow.

Naṣer-e Khosraw, *Book of Travels (Safarnama)*, trans. W. M. Thackston Jr. (Albany, N.Y.: Bibliotheca Persica, 1986), 23, 26, 30, 32.

and has a stone roof supported by marble columns. It contains Jesus' cradle, which is made of stone and is large enough for men to pray in. I too prayed there. It is firmly fastened to the floor so that it cannot be moved. This is the cradle the Child Jesus was placed in when he spoke to people.[3] In this mosque the cradle takes the place of the *mehrab*.[4] On the east side is the *mehrab* of Mary and another said to be that of Zachariah. The Koranic verses concerning Zachariah and Mary are inscribed in these niches, and it is said that this was Jesus' birthplace. One of the columns has the imprint of two fingers and looks as though someone had grasped it. They say that when Mary was in labor, she held onto this very column. This mosque is known as Mahd 'Isa [Jesus' Cradle], and many brass and silver lamps are hung here and kept burning throughout the night.

Passing out through the door, again on the east wall at a corner of the large sanctuary area, you see another very beautiful mosque, twice as large as Jesus' Cradle Mosque, called al-Aqsa Mosque. This marks the spot to which God transported Mohammad from Mecca on the night of his heavenly ascent, and thence to heaven, as is mentioned in the Koran: "Praise be unto him, who transported his servant by night, from the sacred temple of Mecca to the farther temples of Jerusalem" (Koran 17:1)[5]

In that place is a skillfully constructed edifice with magnificent carpets and an independent staff who are always attendant. . . .

The mosque complex has been designed so that the platform is in the middle of the court, and the Dome of the Rock in the middle of the platform. It is an octagonal edifice, and each of the eight sides is thirty-three cubits long. There are four doors facing the cardinal points of the compass with one blank wall between each two doors. The whole wall is of masonry twenty cubits in measure. The Rock itself is one hundred ells in circumference, although it is not a perfect shape; that is, it is neither circular nor square, but a rock of irregular form like any mountain stone. . . .

The Rock itself rises to the height of a man above the floor and is surrounded by a marble balustrade to keep people away. It is a bluish rock that no one has ever set foot on. On the *qebla* [*qibla*] side is a depression that looks as though someone's foot had sunk in, as into soft clay, for even the imprint of the toes remains; there are seven such marks. What

[3] An incident described in the Qur'an, 19:23–33.
[4] Or mihrab, a niche in a mosque that indicates the direction of the Ka'ba.
[5] The passage in the Qur'an in fact does not name Jerusalem.

I heard is that Abraham was here, and that when Isaac was a small child he walked there and these are his footprints.

There are always people in the Dome of the Rock as *mojawers*[6] and devotees. The place is nicely furnished with carpets of silk and in the middle of the building is a silver lamp suspended over the Rock by a silver chain. There are many silver lamps here, and on each one is written its weight. They were donated by the sultan of Egypt. As I figured, there were a thousand maunds[7] of silver. I saw one enormous candle, seven cubits long and three spans thick; it was as white as camphor and mixed with ambergris. They said that every year the sultan of Egypt sends many candles, one of which was this one, for it had the sultan's name written in gold letters around the bottom.

This place is the third most holy place of God, and it is well known among those learned in religion that prayer made in Jerusalem is worth twenty-five thousand ordinary prayers. Every prayer said in Medina is worth fifty thousand, and every prayer said in Mecca is worth one hundred thousand. May God grant to all his servants success in attaining this!

[6] People who dwell near a holy site to obtain the blessing of proximity.

[7] A maund is roughly eighty pounds, giving an astonishing total of eighty thousand pounds (not a precise measure but, rather, an attempt to convey the idea of "a whole lot of silver!").

7

A Latin Christian Travel Guide to Jerusalem

ca. 1100

One of the two earliest accounts of the First Crusade is called The Deeds of the Franks. *It probably was completed as early as 1101, and it seems to have gone into wide circulation in 1106. At the end of the historical narrative, the scribes included a brief travel guide to Jerusalem, from which these passages have been excerpted. It is based on badly outdated information. Only some of the sites still existed in Jerusalem at the time of*

"Description of the Holy Places of Jerusalem," in *The Deeds of the Franks and the Other Pilgrims to Jerusalem*, ed. Rosalind Hill (London: T. Nelson, 1962), 98–99.

its publication. Nonetheless, it does show us what crusaders and pilgrims expected to find there and how they expected to express their sense of religiosity.

If anyone from western parts wishes to go to Jerusalem let him hold always to the rising sun, and thus he will find sites for prayer in Jerusalem's places, as noted here.[1]

In Jerusalem there is a little room covered with a single stone where Solomon wrote the book of Wisdom. And there between the temple and the altar the blood of Zechariah was spilled before a shrine.[2] Not far from there is a stone where Jews throughout the years come and weep and wail and depart from it sad. There is the house of Hezekiah, King of Judah, to whose life God added fifteen years.[3] From there is the house of Caiaphas and the column to which Christ was bound and beaten with whips. Next to the Nablus gate is the residence of Pilate, where Christ was judged by the high priests. Not far from there is Golgotha—that is, the place of Calvary—where Christ the Son of God was crucified. There as well the First Adam was buried,[4] and there Abraham sacrificed to God. From there, about a stone's throw to the west, is the place where Joseph of Arimathea buried the Lord's holy body, and there a church was beautifully built by king Constantine. From Mount Calvary it is thirteen feet to the west to the middle of the world.[5] On the left side is a prison where Christ was imprisoned. Near the right side of the Sepulcher is a Latin monastery dedicated to the Holy Virgin Mary, where her home was. There is an altar in that monastery where the Virgin Mother Mary stood along with her mother's sister Mary Cleophas and Mary Magdalene, weeping and crying as they saw the Lord placed on the Cross. There Jesus said to his mother, "Woman, behold your son," and to his disciple, "Behold your mother."[6]

[1] The writer presents Jerusalem as a sort of "East Pole," the easternmost point of the globe. If one follows the sunrise, one inevitably reaches Jerusalem.

[2] See Matthew 23:35, where Christ describes the death of Zechariah.

[3] 2 Kings 20:6.

[4] In the Christian tradition, Christ is known as "the Second Adam." Most medieval travelers believed the original Adam to have been buried in nearby Hebron, but there was a strong tradition that he was buried on the site of the Crucifixion.

[5] According to long-standing tradition held by Jews and Christians, Jerusalem was the center, or navel, of the world. Jews, however, would locate the central point on the Temple Mount rather than inside the Church of the Holy Sepulcher.

[6] John 19:26–27. The disciple is John.

From this place, about two bowshots to the east is the Temple of the Lord made by Solomon,[7] where Christ was presented by Simeon the Just. To the right of this temple, Solomon built his own temple, and between each temple he raised a beautiful portico composed of marble columns.[8] On the left is the Pool of Testing. Facing east, about 1,000 paces away, one can see the Mount of Olives, where Lord Jesus prayed thusly to the Father: "Father, if it is possible," etc.[9] Between the Temple of the Lord and the Mount of Olives is the Valley of Jehoshaphat, where the Virgin Mary was buried by the apostles. In this valley the Lord will come to judge the world. Nearby is the village called Gethsemane, and nearby, across the Kidron torrent, is the garden where Judas betrayed Jesus. Nearby is the tomb of the prophet Isaiah.

[7] The Latin Christian name for the Dome of the Rock; see also Luke 2:26.

[8] The author describes here the Dome of the Rock and al-Aqsa Mosque, which he believed to be ancient Jewish buildings rather than works of Islamic architecture.

[9] The rest of the verse describing Christ's prayer in the Garden of Gethsemane reads, "Let this cup pass from me. Yet not as I will but as you will" (Matthew 26:39).

8

A Map of Jerusalem from the Time of the Crusades

Twelfth Century

In this map, Jerusalem is portrayed as a perfect circle. The Holy Sepulcher is in the lower left-hand section of the circle. The Temple Mount, with the Dome of the Rock and al-Aqsa Mosque, are in the upper half. Pilgrims appear on the left-hand side of the city; warriors fight below it.

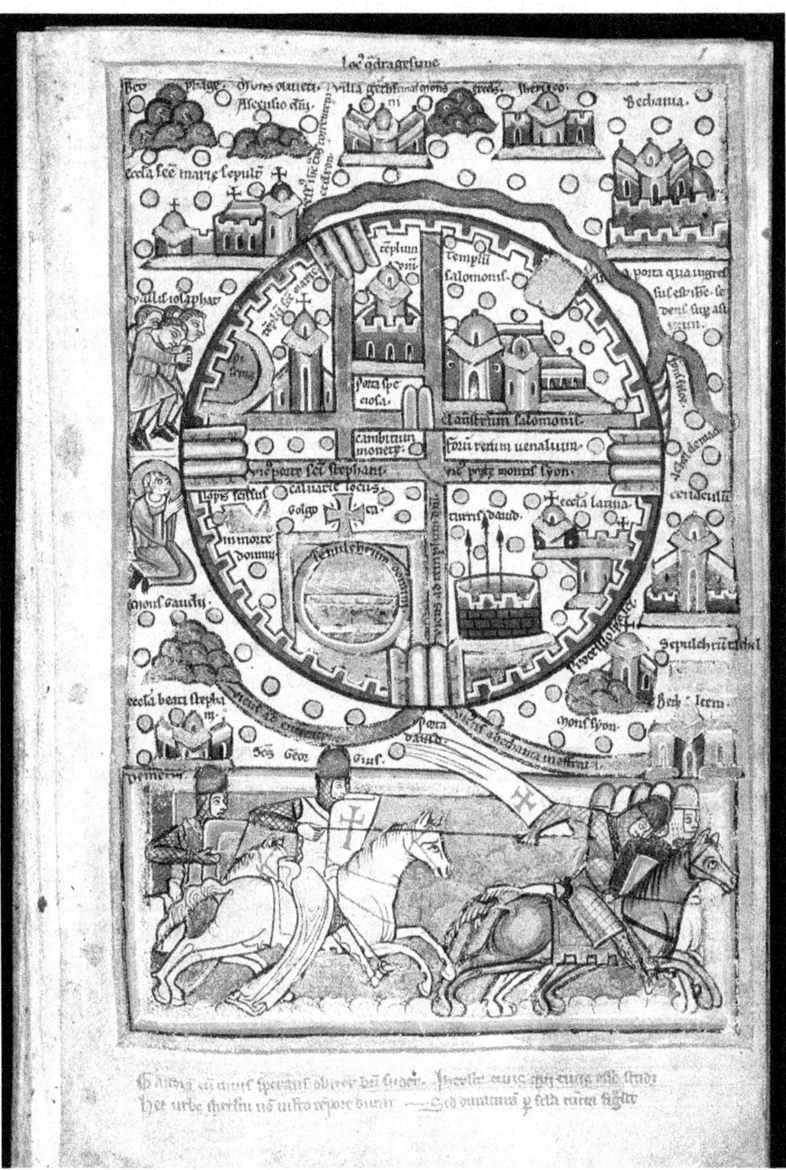
Bethania.
calvarie locus.
mons syon.
cenaculu

9

PSEUDO-METHODIUS

The Revelation of Pseudo-Methodius: Christian Prophecy about Jerusalem and the Apocalypse

ca. 700

The prophecies of Pseudo-Methodius, originally composed in Syriac around the year 700, were not just a prediction of future events. The anonymous author also gives readers a sweeping world history, which is divided into six ages of roughly one thousand years each. His story thus moves from the creation to the end of the world, in the process transitioning from history to prophecy. The excerpts here are from a version of the text that seems to have been written around the time of the First Crusade; this version was updated from the original, earlier text to better reflect current events.

We know, dearest brothers, how in the beginning of the world God created heaven and earth, and through Him all things were created. We know how He made man and a helpmate similar to him and placed them in paradise, and how He called their names Adam and Eve. But then, deceived by the serpent, they were cast out of paradise as virgins. Thirty years later they gave birth to their first children, Cain and his sister Calmana. And after thirty-two years, they gave birth to Abel and his sister Deborah. In year 132 of Adam's life, Cain killed Abel and placed his hand over him. In year 133 of Adam's life, a son was born in his likeness named Seth, a true giant of a man. Then Adam and Eve had other sons and daughters. In year 600 of Adam's life, the sons of Cain molested their brothers' wives, and in year 800 of Adam's life, Cain's sons spread fornication and impurity all over the earth. At age 930, Adam died and was buried in Hebron during the world's first millennium. Then the tribe of Seth divided from the tribe of Cain, and Seth took his tribe to a mountain in the east immediately next to paradise. Cain and his people settled in the same place where he had committed his wicked murder, in India,

---

Based on a transcription of Manuscript Bibliothèque nationale de France *lat.* 13700, 144v–149r. Translated by the author.

and there Cain founded the first city, whose name he called Effrem.[1] All this happened before the flood. In the fortieth year of Jared's life, the world completed the first millennium.[2]

[After describing the next three thousand years of history, Methodius reaches the fifth millennium and a topic closer to the crusades: the fate of the children of Ishmael, the son of the Jewish patriarch Abraham.]

In year twenty-five of the fifth millennium, King Sampsisahid came down from Eoa[3] with a great army and massacred the peoples of the seventy-eight cities of that land and traveled as far as the Third Kingdom of India. After leaving India, he went to Arabia and traveled into the Saba desert and the land of the Ishmaelites. There he set his camps in the lands of the sons of Ishmael, and there King Sampsisahid was conquered by the Saracens.[4] Many thousands fell there or fled.

And then for the first time the sons of Ishmael left the deserts to make wars against the kingdoms of men, just as God had promised to Ishmael, when He said that Ishmael would fix his tents in the land of his brothers.[5] Their camps were a great multitude, and they set forth to fight against lands to the east and the south. They devastated cities and built a navy and traveled into western parts near Rome and brought lands under their power for a time. They nourished themselves on the flesh of camels and drank the blood of oxen mixed with milk and made for themselves four princes: Oreb, Zeeb, Zebah, and Zalmuna.[6] But when they happened upon the sons of Israel, the Lord struck them there and bound them over into the hands of Gideon, son of Joash the Abiezrite. There were 140,000 men, but their princes fell there

[1] Genesis 4:17 says that Cain founded a city called Enoch. According to St. Augustine's famous vision of history, mankind is on a journey from the City of Man, originally founded by Cain, to the City of God—heaven, whose image in this world is Jerusalem.

[2] Though frowned upon by church fathers, the belief that world history was divided into roughly six millennia, with the world ending in the year 6000, remained popular at this time.

[3] A mythical Eastern land that, according to Methodius, was settled by Noah's fourth son, Jonitus.

[4] *Saracen* was a catchall term used by Latin Christians for Muslims. They claimed that Arabs liked to call themselves Saracens, intended to imply that they were "descended from Sarah," Abraham's wife, since they were ashamed of being the offspring of the slave Hagar. Saba is an alternate name for the Judean desert.

[5] Genesis 16:12.

[6] The names of Midianite princes mentioned in the Old Testament (Judges 7). The Midianites were legendarily descendants of Abraham's son Midian by his wife Keturah (Genesis 25:1–2), not sons of Ishmael.

and Gideon pursued them back into their own country, and thus God freed the sons of Israel from enslavement to the sons of Ishmael. But they will come again and make the land destitute and obtain dominion over the whole world. . . .

In the sixth and current millennium,[7] the sons of Ishmael will come out of the desert, and their advent shall be a punishment without measure or mercy. And God will turn over into their hands the kingdoms of all the nations of the earth, because of the sins and the deeds we have done against his commands. Thus God gives us over into the hands of barbarians, because they stain themselves with so many wicked deeds that it is disgusting to speak of it. Therefore God gives them over into the hands of Saracens. Persia will be enslaved and massacred. Cappadocia will be enslaved and massacred. Sicily will be in their control. The land of Syria will lie devastated, its people made prisoners. The people of Cilicia will similarly die by the sword.[8] Greece will be enslaved and massacred. The same with Africa. Egypt and East Asia will become tributary states, forced to pay a huge burden of silver and gold. Spain will fall by the sword and become their prisoner. Parts of Gaul, Germany, and Aquitaine will be swallowed up in various battles, and many of its people made prisoners. The Romans will be massacred and turned to flight, and the islands of the sea will be desolated. And the sons of Ishmael will control the passes from the north and east and west and south, and Jerusalem will be filled with people led there as captives, and together they will cover the Promised Land.

Their yoke will lie heavy on all peoples, and all things will be under their yoke. Everything they shall claim as tribute, and the ornaments of the heavens shall be theirs. And all the splendors once in the churches of the saints—gold or silver or precious stones—will be theirs, and they will scatter the servants of God, both princes and people, for the churches they shall burn. Great will be the tribulation. They will cast bodies into public squares and will not bury them. The way of the Saracens shall stretch from sea to sea, and there will be lands with no path, and their road will be called "the way of misery." Servants alongside the elderly, rich and poor, will take this path, and they will cry out in their

[7] The sixth millennium is not just chronological (referring to the five thousandth to the six thousandth years of the existence of the world) but also conceptual. It is the age of the church and the last age of world history. Despite injunctions to the contrary, some early medieval theologians attempted to calculate when the year 6000 would happen and hence when the world would end.

[8] Cappadocia, Syria, and Cilicia together comprised much of the territory between Constantinople and Jerusalem covered by the First Crusade.

suffering and sadness, "Blessed are those who passed from this light before us!"

This is what Blessed Paul predicted when he said that first there will be a falling away and that at that time the man of sin, the son of perdition, will be revealed.[9] What is this "falling away" except a punishment by which the sons of Ishmael seize control of all the people of world? This is why God prophetically called their father Ishmael "a wild ass." Like a wild ass or a goat or all manner of beasts from the desert, they steal from the flock.[10] They are not men like earlier generations, but they are sons born of the desert, detestable to other men. Listen now to the précis of those who shall come from the desert.

Women about to give birth they will stab with a sword, killing mother and child at once. Priests they will kill in front of the shrines of saints, and in the saints' churches they will have sex with women. They and their wives will wear the sacred vestments of churches. Their beasts of burden they shall lead to the tombs of saints as if to a stable. And there will be a great tribulation among the Christians who live in their lands, and then those who will be steadfast in their faith in Christ shall make themselves known. God will not send these tribulations so that the just believers in Christ might suffer, but rather to reveal the ones numbered among the faithful. As the Truth says, "Blessed are those who suffer in my name—etc."[11] Thus were persecuted the prophets who came before you, but whoever perseveres until the end shall be saved.

After the tribulation, when the sons of Ishmael—clad in purple robes decorated with gold and looking like bridegrooms—have spread over the whole earth, they will say, "The Christians cannot escape from our hands!" Glorying in the victories, they will say, "Behold, through our own strength we have conquered the land and all who live in it!"

Then the Lord God, who promised to show mercy to everyone who loves him, will remember the believers in Christ, and he will free them from the hands of the Saracens. For a king of the Christians shall rise up and make war against them, and he will kill them with the sword and lead their women captive and slaughter their children.[12] And the children of Ishmael will fall by the sword amidst tribulation and suffering,

[9] 2 Thessalonians 2:3, a biblical verse widely understood in the Middle Ages to foretell the advent of Antichrist. As interpreted here, the "falling away" is the losses to Christianity caused by the spread of Islam.

[10] The Latin here seems to be a badly mangled version of the already mangled original text. The translation is a bit free-form.

[11] A paraphrase of Matthew 5:11.

[12] This prophetic figure is often called "the Last World Emperor."

and God shall render to them the same evils they made to others, and onto their own heads shall fall seven times the wickedness they inflicted on others. And God will hand them over into the hands of Christians, and the kingdom of Christians shall be exalted above all other kingdoms, and the Christians will place a heavy yoke on them, and those who survive shall be enslaved. Then there will be peace in the lands that the Saracens had destroyed, and the wrath of the King of the Romans will fall heavily on the Egyptian and Arab Christians who had denied Christ. Then shall reign peace and tranquillity over the land, the likes of which there has never been before nor ever will be again. There shall be happiness and peace upon the land, and all shall enjoy a respite from tribulation.

After this time of peace, tranquillity, and security will come sudden destruction. There will be men in those days as in the days of Noah—drinking and eating, celebrating, marrying and breaking the bonds of marriage—and in their hearts there shall be no fear. Then will come Gog and Magog, and where there was peace, the gates in the north at the Caspian Sea will be unlocked and the tribes with Gog and Magog set loose, and all the land will be struck with fear of them.[13] All men who live upon the face of the earth shall feel terror and hide from their sight in mountains and in caves. They shall leave the north as a plague, these descendants of Japeth.[14] These men will eat the flesh of men, and they will chew up serpents, beasts of burden, and women with their children. No one shall be able to resist them. And after seven years, when they have claimed the city of Jaffa,[15] the Lord will send one of his princes, and he will in an instant strike them with lightning and fire. Then the Emperor of the Greeks will come and sit in Jerusalem for seven years.[16]

Then shall appear the son of perdition who is called Antichrist. He will be born in Chorazin and raised in Bethsaida, and will reign in Capernaum.[17] This is why the Lord says in the Gospel, "Woe to you Chorazin! Woe to you, Bethsaida! Woe to you, Capernaum! If you are raised to heaven, you will go down to hell!"[18]

[13] Gog and Magog are names associated in the Bible with the apocalypse. In Pseudo-Methodius, they are barbarian tribes that, along with twenty other tribes, Alexander the Great sealed behind gates in the world's northern climes.

[14] One of the sons of Noah.

[15] A port city near Jerusalem.

[16] Apparently the same figure who struck down Gog and Magog, called elsewhere in this selection the King of the Romans and Greeks.

[17] Chorazin, Bethsaida, and Capernaum were all villages around the Sea of Galilee.

[18] Luke 10:13, 15.

After this, the King of the Romans and Greeks will go up to Golgotha, where the Lord deigned to suffer for us death on the cross.[19] The King of the Romans will raise the crown from his head and place it on the back of his neck while stretching his hands to heaven.[20] Thus the king of the Christians will turn over his spirit to God, and the sign of the cross will appear in heaven.

Then shall come the son of perdition, who shall believe himself to be God. He will work on the earth many signs and wonders: The blind will see, the lame will walk, the deaf will hear, and the dead will seem to rise—all intended to lead the elect into error. He shall enter Jerusalem and will sit in the Temple of God, thinking in his proud heart that he is God, when in fact he is a man, from the seed of man and the son of a woman from the tribe of Dan. He will be deceitful and mendacious. His frauds will mislead many.

God afterward will send his two most faithful servants, Elijah and Enoch, whom he had set aside as witnesses to accuse his enemy.[21] At that time the first will be last, and the Jews will believe.[22] Elijah and Enoch will accuse him before all the people and will show him to be mendacious and deceitful, and he shall be confounded. The peoples will then see him proved a liar and confounded by God's saints. Then the Jews will believe, and 144,000 of all the tribes of Israel shall be killed for Christ in those days. And Antichrist, filled with fury, will order the saints of God killed along with any who believed in them.

Then our Lord Jesus Christ, the Son of the living God, will come in heavenly glory amidst the clouds of the sky surrounded by crowds of angels. With the sword of his mouth he will strike down Antichrist—the beast, the enemy, the seducer—and all those who obey him. This will be the end of the world, and there will be a judgment, in the presence of thousands upon thousands of angels and ten times one hundred thousand archangels, cherubim, and seraphim.

[19] Golgotha, "the place of the skull," is also known as Mount Calvary. In the eleventh century, as today, it was incorporated into the architecture of the Church of the Holy Sepulcher in Jerusalem.

[20] The scene described here is a variation on the medieval ceremony of *chevage*, where a landholder would abase himself before a lord and offer the tax that he owed for his land by placing coins on the back of his neck—a literal head tax. Instead of coins, the king places his crown, sign of dominion over the whole world, on his neck. In the original version of this prophecy, the Last World Emperor placed his crown on a cross, which then rose into heaven.

[21] The two witnesses are unnamed in Revelation 11. Medieval exegetes traditionally identified them as the Old Testament prophets Elijah and Enoch, who did not die but, while alive, were taken directly to heaven by God.

[22] One of the key signs of the Last Days would be the conversion of the Jews to Christianity.

10

RODULFUS GLABER

A French Monk's Account of the Destruction of the Holy Sepulcher

1009

When the Fatimid caliph al-Hakim ordered the destruction of the Church of the Holy Sepulcher, it received relatively little notice in Europe. Those writers who did mention it, however, were deeply shocked. It appeared to them to be not just an act of vandalism but part of a broader anti-Christian conspiracy, with its roots possibly in Europe. In this excerpt, the Burgundian monk Rodulfus Glaber (d. 1047) indicates that rumors of events in Jerusalem sparked cries for vengeance against Christ's enemies wherever they lived and of whatever religion they might hold.

In the same year, the ninth after the aforementioned millennium,[1] the church in Jerusalem that contains the sepulcher of our Lord was entirely destroyed at the command of the prince of Babylon.[2] The occasion of its destruction, which I am about to describe, is known to have happened in this fashion: When great crowds of the faithful were traveling to Jerusalem to visit this famous monument to the Lord, the devil again grew envious and wickedly sought to poison the followers of the true faith through his regular helpers, the Jews.

There was a sizable population of this people living in the royal French city of Orléans, and they were known to be bitterer, bolder, and prouder than the rest of their kind. After holding a council together they wickedly hired a vagrant named Robert, who was pretending to be a pilgrim but was in fact a fugitive serf from the monastery at Moutiers dedicated

[1] This refers to the year 1009. Glaber, who organized his chronicle around the years 1000 and 1033, the millennia of Christ's birth and death, respectively, reports widespread apocalyptic expectations during each of those years.

[2] Babylon was an old name for Cairo, used by medieval writers often as a substitute for Egypt.

Rodulfus Glaber Opera, ed. John France, Neithard Bulst, and Paul Reynolds (Oxford: Oxford University Press, 1989), 132–36. Translated by the author.

to the Blessed Mary. After examining him carefully, they sent him to the prince of Babylon with a letter written onto little pieces of parchment in the Hebrew alphabet. They hid this letter inside the man's iron staff to prevent anyone from stealing it. He then set out to deliver this letter, composed of lies and wickedness, to the aforesaid prince. It said that if the prince did not quickly destroy the revered house of Christians, then he could be sure that Christians would soon occupy his entire kingdom and cost him every bit of his authority.[3]

The prince grew enraged on hearing these things and sent some of his men to Jerusalem, ordering them to destroy the aforesaid temple. When they arrived, they did just as he had commanded, though they had little success when they tried to break apart the hollow tomb of the Sepulcher with crowbars. In the same way they tore down the church of the martyr George in Ramla[4] whose power had until then kept the awed Saracens at bay. It is said that previously the Saracens had often approached it but had always been struck blind.

A little after the temple had been destroyed, as I described, it became clear that the wicked Jews were behind this foul crime. When it became known, Christians everywhere by common consent drove all the Jews from their lands and cities. All Jews were hated, all of them exiled from cities, some cut down by swords, some drowned in rivers, others killed by still other means. Some even committed suicide in sundry fashions of self-destruction. After the Jews had suffered this just form of vengeance, hardly any of them could be found in the whole Roman world.[5] Bishops decreed and forbade Christians anywhere to enter into a business contract with them, and they declared that Jews could only be received if they agreed to be converted through the grace of baptism and to renounce all Jewish custom and practice. Many of them did so, more out of fear of death and love for the present life than out of hope for the joys of eternal life. For all of them who had lied in asking to be made Christian soon afterward returned insolently to their former way of life.

[3] Although much of this story is fanciful, it is a remarkable forecast of the First Crusade.

[4] Ramla is a city about thirty miles northwest of Jerusalem.

[5] Glaber exaggerates the level of persecution. Nonetheless, this is the first documented example of a Jewish pogrom in medieval Europe.

11

AL-MAQRIZI

A Muslim Historian's Account of the Destruction of the Holy Sepulcher

Fourteenth Century

The Fatimid Caliphate came to an end in the twelfth century, leaving relatively few contemporary records for historians to work with. One of our best sources for the age of Caliph al-Hakim (996–1021) is a fourteenth-century scholar named al-Maqrizi, who had access to a more extensive archive than now survives. His description of the destruction of the Holy Sepulcher in 1009 provides an important counterpoint to Latin accounts of the same events. In particular, al-Maqrizi connects the destruction of the church to the fraudulent activities of the church's Christian guardians.

That year Christians went from Egypt to Jerusalem to be present at Easter in the Church of the Holy Sepulchre (al-Qumama),[1] as was customary every year, bringing with them important adornments, much as the Muslims do in going out with the pilgrimage caravan. So al-Hakim asked Khatkin the Dayf al-'Adudi, one of his commanders, about that because of the latter's familiarity with the matter of this church. He responded, "The Christians greatly revere this church and make pilgrimages to it from every country. Kings come to visit, carrying to it great wealth, vestments, curtains, furnishings, candle stands, crosses finely wrought in gold and silver, and vessels of the same. There are in it many things of that type. On the day of Easter, the Christians assemble at the church, setting up crosses and suspending candlesticks on the altar. They attempt to have fire transferred to it by means of elder oil mixed with mercury. It produces for the purpose a bright light that those who see this happen suppose has descended from the heavens."

[1] *Qumama* (dung) sounds like the Arabic word *qiyama* (resurrection), thus the name is an unflattering pun for "Church of the Resurrection."

Paul E. Walker, *Caliph of Cairo: Al-Hakim bi-Amr Allah, 996–1021* (Cairo: American University in Cairo Press, 2009), 75.

Al-Hakim rejected that and directed Bishr ibn Surin, the clerk of the chancery, to write to Ahmad b. Ya'qub, the *da'i*,[2] commanding him to proceed straightaway to Jerusalem to destroy the church and have the people plunder it so thoroughly all traces of it were obliterated. He did exactly that. Subsequently, al-Hakim gave an order to raze the churches and synagogues located in the various districts of his kingdom. But, fearing that the Christians would destroy the mosques of the Muslims located in their countries, he refrained from having that done.

[2] The *da'i* is an official responsible for administering the *da'wa*, or call to allegiance, in this case a proclamation of political and religious loyalty to al-Hakim.

12

The Departure of the Great German Pilgrimage of 1064

ca. 1125

In 1064, a mass pilgrimage to Jerusalem departed from Germany amid great prophetic expectation. According to an old tradition, the apocalypse would occur on the feast of Easter during a year in which the Annunciation, which always falls on March 25, coincided with Good Friday, which varies according to conjunctions of the solar and lunar calendars. The text here was written around 1125 in honor of Bishop Altmann of Passau (d. 1091), one of the participants in the pilgrimage.

At this time many nobles were going to Jerusalem to see the Lord's Sepulcher, deceived by a then common idea that Judgment Day was at hand and that it would happen on Easter, when the Resurrection of Christ is marked as in that year on March 27. This terror moved not only common folk but also princes of the people, famous because of their family and rank. Even bishops from various cities, elevated in their great glory and their high office, set aside their relations and

Vita Altmanni Episcopi Pataviensis, Monumenta Germaniae Historica, *Scriptores* 12 (Hannover: Hahnsche, 1856), 230. Translated by the author.

their wealth to follow Christ, carrying the cross along this difficult path. Among them the leading bishop and catalyst was Bishop Gunther of Bamberg, a man famous for his wisdom, equally attractive in body and mind. Many famous men, clerics and laymen, accompanied him, from both East Francia and Bavaria. These included two outstanding canons: the schoolmaster Ezzo, who was gifted with tremendous wisdom and eloquence, who on this very journey would admirably compose in his native tongue a canticle on the miracles of Christ; and Conrad, outstanding in knowledge and in oratory, who afterward would become a prelate to the canons in our church. To these men Altmann would become a companion on the journey and a friend in their toil, departing from the queen's court and bringing with him many distinguished men from the palace.[1]

Having thus undertaken the difficult pilgrimage path, they endured many snares set by the pagans[2] and lost many of their companions and their possessions. How awful! Christ's enemies attacked from behind Christ's priests. Urging their horses on with spears, they drove them about the field of battle. During this journey a particularly memorable event occurred that I will include here as an example—it might frighten anyone whose obstinate mind would otherwise resist the counsel of the wise. Accompanying this journey was a noble abbess of graceful body and of a religious outlook. Setting aside the care of the sisters committed to her and against the advice of the wise, she undertook this great and dangerous pilgrimage. The pagans captured her, and in the sight of all, these shameless men raped her until she breathed her last, to the dishonor of all Christians. Christ's enemies performed such abuses and others like them on the Christians and thus transformed them into a spectacle for angels and men, since they had chosen to pass through many tribulations that they might enter the kingdom of God.

[1] Altmann, who had been educated in the cathedral school in Paderborn, was a courtier to the German emperor Henry III. He would become bishop of Passau upon his return from Jerusalem.

[2] Bands of Seljuk Turks who were conducting raids in Fatimid territory.

13

LAMBERT OF HERSFELD

The Crisis of the German Pilgrimage, March 27, 1065

Twelfth Century

The pilgrims sought shelter in an abandoned fortress, to which the Turks, driven by a desire for plunder, lay siege. Rescue from the Seljuk Turks would come from an entirely unexpected source: the Fatimid Caliphate. The following account was written by a German monk named Lambert, who himself had been a pilgrim to Jerusalem in 1058/59.

After three days,[1] exhausted by suffering and hunger, [the pilgrims] had reached their breaking point. Their strength sapped, they had failed in all their exertions and efforts. Then one of their priests told them that they were not acting rightly, that they were putting their hope and strength in their weapons rather than in God, and that they were trying by their own powers to escape tribulations into which God had allowed them to fall. It was now a better plan to surrender, especially since the past three days of fighting had left them helpless. It would not be difficult for God to grant them mercy and liberate them miraculously, trapped as they were on every side, if they surrendered and placed themselves under the enemy's yoke. He added this: that their enemies had tormented them not for the sake of killing them but so that they might take their money. If they obtained money, they might let them go free and unharmed, without suffering any further punishment.

This counsel pleased everyone, and right away they turned from weapons to prayer. Through an interpreter they made a pleading offer of surrender. When the Arab duke heard about it, he called for his horse and gathered together his most important men. The rest he ordered to

[1] March 27, which was Easter—meaning that the anticipated apocalypse had not arrived.

Lambert of Hersfeld, *Annales*, ed. O. Holder-Egger, Monumenta Germaniae Historica, *Scriptores rerum Germanicarum in usum scholarum* 38 (Hannover: Hahnsche, 1894), 95–98. Translated by the author.

stay behind, fearing that if all his people entered the city at once, they might recklessly give themselves over to plunder. Taking with him seventeen of his most distinguished men, he entered the now open fortress. At the gates he left his son to act as a guard, lest someone he had not chosen greedily burst into the city after him. Ladders were lowered into place, and the duke and a few of his men climbed into the upper room where the bishops of Mainz and Bamberg were sequestered. Everyone had decided to give the privilege of speaking to the bishop of Bamberg, although he was the younger man, on account of his exemplary physical appearance and his extraordinary merits. The bishop thus asked the duke that he allow the pilgrims to depart stripped of possessions, saying that they would surrender all their property down to the last penny.

The duke, as he considered the defeat his legions had scored, was both elated at the victory and unhinged even beyond the usual innate savagery of his people. He said that, to his way of thinking, he had waged war now for three days, and not without significant losses to his army. In place of the terms that the defeated Christians had offered him, therefore, he would impose these conditions. Lest false hope deceive them, he would first take everything that they had, and then he would eat their flesh and drink their blood. Without pause he took the cloth that he wore on his head in the custom of that nation and made out of it a chain and cast it around the bishop's neck. The bishop, who was a courteous, soft-spoken man of serious demeanor, could not bear this insult. He hit the duke in the head with such a blow that this one punch knocked him headlong to the floor. Bishop Gunther shouted as he did so that he would punish the man's impiety for daring to raise profane and idolatrous hands against one of Christ's priests.

The rest of the clerics and laymen piled onto the duke and the others who had accompanied him into the upper room, and they bound their hands behind their backs with chains so tight that their skin broke in several places and blood dripped down from their fingernails. They signaled what they had boldly done to those who had stayed in the lower part of the building, so that they could dish out the same treatment to the Arab princes who were still with them. Then all the laymen raised a shout to heaven and called for help to God, the maker of all things. Once again they took up their weapons, resumed their places on the city walls, and with a small band pounced on the troops which were near the gates and put them to flight. They carried out this plan quickly, so reinvigorated by this unexpected turn of events that you would have thought them to have suffered no fatigue, no hardship from their three days of fasting and suffering.

The Arabs wondered greatly at this sudden burst of activity born of desperation and unforeseen developments. Not suspecting the cause—that punishment had been inflicted on their princes—they quickly turned their minds to battle and called the troops to arms, preparing to burst through the guards and into the fortress. And so it would have happened, if the Christians had not quickly taken counsel and perched the conquered princes in the very places where the enemies were fiercely attacking them, raining down a dense torrent of spears. A scout stood over their heads holding an unsheathed sword in his hands, and he called out through an interpreter that unless the Arabs ceased from their attack, then the pilgrims would batter them not with weapons but with the heads of their princes. Then these same princes, feeling the weight of the sword on their necks as much as the weight of the chains, entreated their men loudly to move with care and not to enrage their enemies, because a reckless attack would bring them only suffering and death and cut off all hope of mercy.

The Arab duke's son, who, as I mentioned earlier, had been left to defend the gate by his father, felt stunned at the danger his father now faced. He ran into the midst of his men's closely packed ranks and berated them with words and gestures, restraining the army's violent impulses and ordering them not to throw any more spears at their enemies, for their spears would strike not the breasts of their enemies, as they intended, but rather their own leaders would receive the blows.

During this respite from arms and conflict, a messenger for the Christians entered the fortress—a man whom they had sent to Ramla on Good Friday when they had been naked and wounded. To minds yet seasoned with bitterness and fear, this messenger brought great comfort. He explained that, apparently, a divine impulse had overcome the Duke of Ramla, even though he was a pagan, to come with many soldiers and free them.[2] And the news of his imminent arrival was not lost on the Arabs. Immediately their thoughts turned from attacking others to saving themselves. They fell into headlong flight, each of them driven by hope of escape. In the midst of this frenzied activity, as some people rushed to look after other matters, one of the prisoners escaped with the help of a Saracen whom the Christians had employed as a guide. This caused so much sadness and grief among the Christians that they were hardly able to restrain their hands from striking him through whose indulgence the prisoner had been sent away.

[2] The author does not understand the distinction between Turks and Fatimids and is therefore confused about why one group of pagans would oppose another.

Not long afterward, the Duke of Ramla arrived with his army, just as predicted, and the Christians, caught between hope and fear that they would suffer some other catastrophe, peacefully received him at the city's entry. But the enemy had changed. The strangeness of the thing makes it difficult to believe. Satan cast out Satan. That is, a pagan wished to prevent another pagan from attacking Christians. First the duke ordered everyone in chains to be brought before him. When he had seen them and had heard in order what had happened, he thanked the Christians heartily for what they had done fighting against his commonwealth's bitter foes. For years now these men had attacked the kingdom of Babylon with frequent raids, and in battle they had often routed the great armies he had sent against them. He commanded that the captives be kept alive to be confined in the King of Babylon's prisons. In exchange for a suitable gift of money, he led the Christians with him to Ramla. From there, he ordered that they be led to Jerusalem, accompanied by young men chosen to protect them, lest they suffer further harassment from bandits.

14

A Replica in Bologna of the Holy Sepulcher

Late Eleventh Century

Constructed around the time of the First Crusade, this replica of the Edicule (the small building within the larger Church of the Holy Sepulcher that contains the tomb of Christ) replicates more closely the appearance of the goal of the First Crusade than does the current Edicule in Jerusalem.

Scala / Art Resource, N.Y.

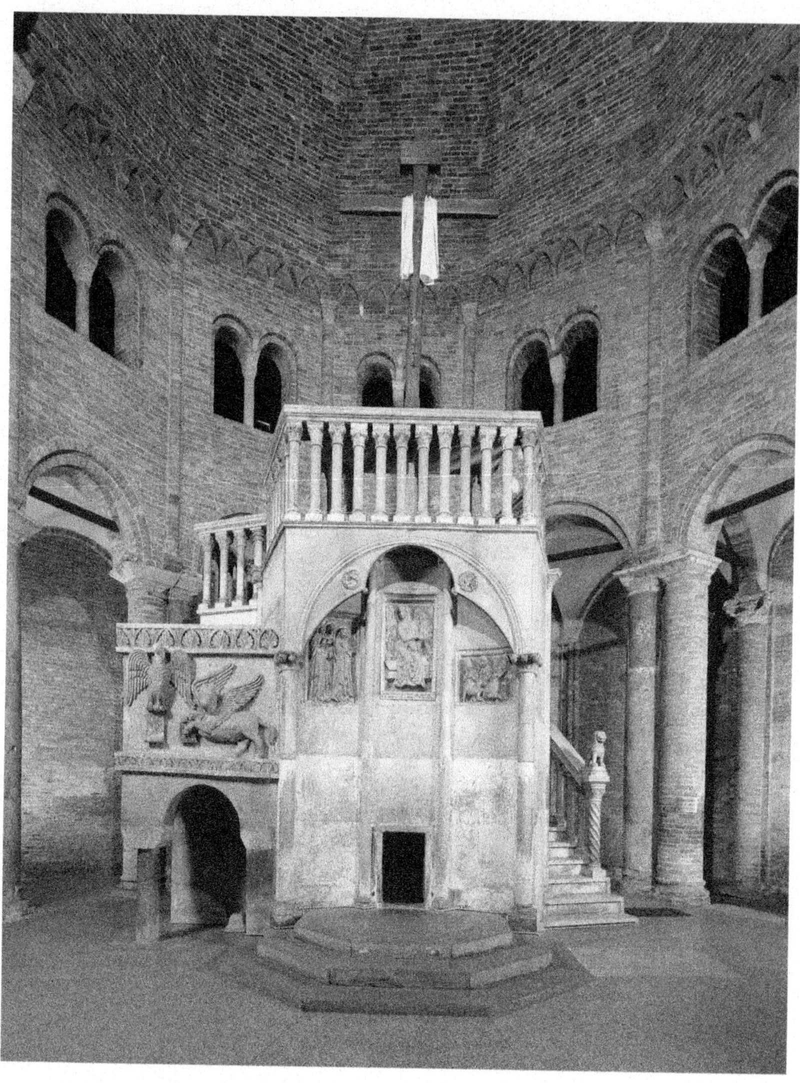

3

The Call to Crusade

15

BISHOP LAMBERT OF ARRAS

Urban II's Crusading Indulgence

1095

Several contemporary historians composed versions of what Urban II preached at Clermont, but none of them is entirely reliable. The only sure sentence about the crusade to survive from Clermont—preserved in a collection of decrees by Bishop Lambert of Arras, who attended the council—is notable for its brevity and for the qualifications that it places on the promise of indulgence. As such, it merits careful reading.

Whoever shall set forth to liberate the church of God at Jerusalem for the sake of devotion alone and not to attain honor or money will be able to substitute that journey for all penance.

Robert Somerville, *The Councils of Urban II: Decreta Claromontensia* (London: Adolf M. Hakkert, 1972), 1:74.

16

ROBERT THE MONK

Urban II's Sermon at Clermont: The Version of Robert the Monk

ca. 1107

Robert the Monk was one of three northern French monastic writers who, around 1107, rewrote the anonymous eyewitness account of the First Crusade, The Deeds of the Franks. *Robert did so in part because he had attended the Council of Clermont—though he was not necessarily interested in giving an accurate presentation of the pope's words. Rather, he wished to give his own interpretation of the crusade and in particular of the enemies whom the Franks would face in the Holy Land.*

In the year of our Lord 1095 a great council was held in the region of the Auvergne in Gaul, in a city known as Clermont. Pope Urban II presided over the meeting with bishops and cardinals. That council was renowned for bringing together both Gauls and Germans, and as many bishops as lay princes attended. When the ecclesiastical affairs were settled, the Lord Pope went into an open field. No single building could hold all those people. There he pronounced these beautiful and compelling words, in this fashion, to everyone gathered there:

"Frankish people! People from across the mountains! Splendid in so many deeds, people chosen and loved by God, distinguished from all other nations by the quality of your lands, the purity of your faith, and the honor that Holy Church has given to you, to you my sermon is directed and to you I offer my entreaty!

"From the lands around Jerusalem and the city of Constantinople, troubling news has arisen and many times has now come to our attention—namely, that the people of the kingdom of Persia, a foreign people, a people entirely hostile to God, *a generation whose heart was not steadfast and whose spirit has not kept faith with God,*[1] has attacked Christian

[1] Psalms 78:8.

Robert of Reims, *Historia Hierosolimitana,* in Recueil des Historiens des Croisades, *Historiens occidentaux* 3 (Paris: Imprimerie Royale, 1866), 727–31. Translated by the author.

lands and devastated them with sword, plunder, and fire. Some of the captives they have led into their own land, while others they have laid low with a wretched death. The churches of God they have altogether overthrown or enslaved to their own cult. The altars they have wrecked, polluted with their filth; for they circumcise Christians and either pour the blood from the circumcision over the altars or else use it to fill baptismal vessels. And if it amuses them to punish someone with a truly foul death, they puncture his navel and pull out the ends of his intestines. These they bind to a pole, and then by whipping their victim, they force him to run around and around until his intestines have all come out and he falls dead to the ground. Some they tie to poles and shoot with arrows; others they force to stretch out their bare necks so that with their swords they can cut off their heads in a single blow. What can I say about the wicked violations of women? To speak of it is worse than to keep silent. The kingdom of the Greeks they have so eviscerated and claimed for their own that you could not cross the lands they have taken from them in a journey of two months.

"Who shall avenge these deeds? Upon whom shall fall the burden if not you? To you more than all other people God has conferred great fame at arms, great physical skills, and strength for laying low the hairy scalp of the enemy.[2]

"May the deeds of your ancestors move you and fill your minds with valor—the wisdom and magnificence of King Charlemagne and his son Louis and all your other kings who destroyed pagan kingdoms and spread far and wide the bounds of Holy Church.[3] You should be especially moved thinking on the Holy Sepulcher of our Lord and Savior and on the other sacred places, now in the clutches of this most foul people. Unworthily they touch them, and sacrilegiously they pollute them with their filth.

"O strongest knights, offspring of indomitable forebears, do not decline from their standards, but rather remember your ancestors' examples! If perhaps the love of your children or your parents or your wives should hold you back, recall what the Lord says in the Gospel: *Who loves his father or mother more than me is not worthy of me. Whoever abandons his home or father or mother or wife or children or lands because of my name will win it back hundredfold through eternal life.*[4]

[2] See Psalms 67:21.

[3] The Frankish king Charlemagne (r. 768–814) enjoyed a largely undeserved reputation in the eleventh century for leading wars against Muslims. His son and successor was Louis the Pious (r. 814–840).

[4] Matthew 10:37 and 19:29.

"Let none of your possessions nor any of your daily tasks restrain you! For this land that you inhabit, surrounded on all sides by sea and mountain, is choking under your great multitude. It has no real riches and provides barely enough food for its farmers. That is why you fight and kill one another, you wage wars and you mortally wound so many people. Let the hatreds that separate you cease! Let your feuds be settled! Let your wars calm and your quarrels and controversies be pacified. Take the path of the Holy Sepulcher, retake that land from so wicked a people, subdue to your will this territory given by God into the possession of the sons of Israel, *flowing with milk and honey*, just as the Bible says.[5]

"Jerusalem is the navel of the world, a land fertile beyond all others, as if another paradise of delights. The Redeemer of the human race glorified it with his presence, enhanced it with his sermons, sanctified it with his passion, redeemed it by his death, and distinguished it through his burial. This is a royal city, placed at the center of the world, now held captive by her enemies, enslaved by a gentile people ignorant of the worship of God. She wishes and desires to be freed, never ceasing to plead for rescue. She especially demands help from you, since, as I have already said, God has set you aside before all other nations because of your skills at war. Take this path, then, for the remission of your sins, confident in the imperishable glory of the heavenly kingdom!"

With these words and many others like them, Pope Urban urbanely preached his sermon, such that the hearts of all those present came together as one and proclaimed, "God wills it! God wills it!" Hearing this outcry, the venerable Roman bishop turned his eyes to heaven, gave thanks to God, and raising his hands for silence said: "Dear brethren, today is made plain for us what the Lord said in the Gospel: *When two or three of you are gathered together in my name, I am in your midst.*[6] If the Lord God was not in your minds, you would have not joined together in one voice. Although there were many voices, they originated from one only. Therefore I say to you that God put this into your heart and caused you to say this. Let these words therefore become for you a battle cry in the midst of combat, for the words come from God. When you join together and strike against the enemy, let this single divine rallying cry unite you all: 'God wills it! God wills it!'

"Additionally, we order and encourage the old and the sickly, barely suited to carrying arms, not to set out on this road. Women without

[5] Exodus 3:8.
[6] Matthew 18:20.

husbands or brothers or legal guardians should not set forth either. People like that will be more of a hindrance than a help, more a burden than a benefit. The wealthier should aid the less fortunate and should take with them men whom they themselves have equipped for war. Priests and clerics of any order cannot depart without the permission of their bishops, because this road will prove useless to them if they go without sanction, just as laymen derive no benefit from a pilgrimage without the blessing of their priest. Whoever sets his mind and vows to God to go on this holy pilgrimage, promising freely to offer himself as a living sacrifice, holy and pleasing to God, shall put the sign of the cross on his brow or his chest. When he fulfills his vow and wishes to return, let him place the cross on his back between his shoulders. By this twofold procedure they will have fulfilled the Lord's command given in the Gospel: *Whoever does not take up his cross and follow me is not worthy of me.*"[7]

[7] Luke 14:27.

17

GUIBERT OF NOGENT

Urban II's Sermon at Clermont: An Excerpt from Guibert of Nogent's Version

ca. 1107

Guibert of Nogent is another of the French monks who wrote a crusade chronicle around 1107. His style is more deliberately elevated than Robert the Monk's (see Document 16), and Guibert infused his narrative with a much higher theological diction. Like Robert, Guibert used Urban's sermon as a vehicle for advancing his interpretation of the meaning of the crusade. Unlike Robert, he did not attend the Council of Clermont.

Guibert of Nogent, *Dei gesta per Francos*, ed. R. B. C. Huygens, Corpus Christianorum Continuatio Mediaevalis 127A (Turnhout: Brepols, 1996), 113–16. Translated by the author.

"Now you need to think carefully about this: that if God is working with you as his agents to cause Christian worship to flourish again at that church that is the mother of all churches, he perhaps is doing so to restore some parts of the East to the faith against the oncoming time of Antichrist. Obviously, Antichrist is going to arise to make war not against Jews, not against gentiles, but—as the etymology of his name suggests—against Christians; and if Antichrist finds no Christians in that part of the world where hardly any are today, there won't be anyone for him to oppose and no one whom he might rightly challenge. According to Daniel and to Daniel's interpreter Jerome,[1] Antichrist will fix his tents on the Mount of Olives, and we know through the Apostle that he will sit in the temple of God in Jerusalem as if he were a god.[2] From the same prophet we learn that Antichrist will kill three great kings—of Egypt, Africa, and Ethiopia—undoubtedly because of their Christian faith. But this obviously cannot happen unless Christianity appears where now there is only paganism. If you dedicate yourself to the task of righteous battles, therefore, so that you (who have accepted from Jerusalem the seedbed of the knowledge of God) might fully restore the debt of grace once paid there, and so that through you the Catholic name might be spread against the wickedness of Antichrist and his Anti-Christians, who then could help but conclude that God, who exceeds the hopes of all through his bountiful goodness, might consume the reeds of paganism through that spark that you will light? Thus God might bring under the rudiments of our law Egypt, Africa, and Ethiopia, now separated from the communion of our faith, so that Antichrist, the sinner, the son of perdition, might find there enemies ranged against him.

"Listen also how the Gospel proclaims that Jerusalem shall be downtrodden *by peoples until the times of nations are fulfilled.*[3] 'Times of nations' can be understood in two ways. It could mean that *the nations* have willfully lorded it over Christians and have wallowed in the pigsties of their own lusts and impurities, all the while experiencing no opposition (for to 'have one's time' is said of a person who attains anything he desires; hence the verse, *My time has not yet come, your time is always at hand,* and hence it is said of pleasure seekers, *You are having*

[1] Daniel is the Old Testament prophet whose book provided much material for apocalyptic speculation. His "interpreter" was St. Jerome (ca. 347–420), who translated the Bible into Latin and whose works include a commentary on Daniel.

[2] 2 Thessalonians 2:3–4.

[3] Luke 21:24.

your time).[4] Alternatively, 'times of nations' refers to the full number of people to enter the faith before Israel will be saved.[5] These 'times,' dearest brothers, may perhaps only be fulfilled through your agency and under God's direction when the pagan powers are repulsed. And now, as the end of time approaches, these people have not been converted because, according to the Apostle, there must first be a falling away from the faith.[6] Nevertheless, it is necessary according to the prophets that before the advent of Antichrist, Christian rule must be renewed in those parts of the world, either through you or through whomever it pleases God to use. In that way the head of all evil, who will have a throne there, will find some fodder of the faith against which he might strike.

"Just think what the Almighty may have prepared for you! Through you he might restore Jerusalem from its downtrodden state! I ask you to consider what joys might fill your hearts if we should see the holy city raised up through your help and thus prophecies—no! more truly, divine oracles—fulfilled in our times! Remember what the Lord himself said in his own voice: *From the East I will lead your seed, and from the West I will gather you*.[7] God 'led our seed from the East' because, in a dual fashion, those Eastern lands produced the beginnings of our church, but in the West he gathers the church together because those Westerners, who after the Easterners accepted the lessons of the faith, will restore the losses of Jerusalem. We think that by God's help this can happen through you."

[4] The first expression is from John 7:6; the second appears to have been proverbial only.

[5] Romans 11:25–26.

[6] 2 Thessalonians 2:3.

[7] Isaiah 43:5.

18

ALBERT OF AACHEN

Peter the Hermit as Inventor of the Crusade

ca. 1107

The passage presented here is taken from the crusade chronicle of Albert of Aachen, who probably began writing his chronicle around the same time as Robert the Monk and Guibert of Nogent wrote theirs (see Documents 16 and 17). Like Robert and Guibert, Albert did not participate in the crusade. His chronicle is nonetheless valuable because it offers a Germanic perspective on the campaign, based on now lost written and oral sources and on eyewitness testimony as well. Albert also differs from his French counterparts because he credits the wandering preacher Peter the Hermit rather than Urban II with being the inventor of the crusade and its most important advocate.

There was a priest named Peter, once a hermit, born in the city of Amiens in the western part of the kingdom of the Franks. After becoming a preacher in that same kingdom in the region of Berry, he advocated in his every sermon and exhortation, to the best of his ability and before anyone else had done so, for a commitment to this journey. At his constant entreaty and invocation, bishops, abbots, clerics, monks, and finally noble secular princes from various regions—indeed, all commoners whether celibate, married, adulterers, murderers, thieves, perjurers, bandits, and every sort of Christian person, including women—led by penance cheerfully embraced this road. On what occasion and with what intention the hermit preached this path, and how he stood as its originator, this chapter will explain.

Some years before the beginning of the journey, the priest Peter had gone to Jerusalem for the sake of prayer, but when he reached the oratory of the Lord's Sepulcher, he saw many forbidden and wicked things occurring there. His spirit mourned, and he called on God to avenge the crimes he had witnessed. Finally, moved by these wicked deeds,

---

Albert of Aachen, *Historia Ierosolimitana, History of the Journey to Jerusalem*, ed. and trans. Susan B. Edgington (Oxford: Oxford University Press, 2007), 2–4. Translated by the author.

he sought out the patriarch of the holy church of Jerusalem[1] and asked why gentiles and evil men were able to pollute holy places and steal away offerings from the faithful, using the church as if a stable, beating up Christians, despoiling pilgrims through unjust fees, and inflicting on them many sufferings.

Upon hearing these words, the patriarch, a distinguished priest of the Lord's Sepulcher, answered reverently and tearfully, "O you most faithful of Christians! Why do you reprimand me and disturb me in the midst of my fatherly cares? I have but the strength and power of a tiny ant when compared to those proud men. We have to redeem our lives here by regular tribute payments or else face death-dealing punishment, all the time expecting still greater dangers—unless we get help from fellow Christians. Might you perhaps accept this mission?"

Peter answered in this way: "Venerable father, I have heard enough and now I understand and see the weak position of the Christians living here with you and how much misery you suffer from the gentiles. Because of all this and for the grace of God and for your liberation, as God is my companion and as long as I am granted to live, I shall return where I came from and seek out the lord pope, and then all the Christian bishops, kings, dukes, counts, and leaders of principalities. I shall make known the yoke of your servitude and your unbearable suffering. I have seen these things so that I might be able to spread this message."

Later, as heavenly shadows lay across the land, Peter returned to the Holy Sepulcher to pray. There, exhausted by prayers and vigils, he drifted into sleep and in a vision saw the majesty of Lord Jesus, who deigned to speak to this feeble, mortal man. "Peter, beloved Christian son, when you wake up you must go to our patriarch and accept from him a letter sealed with a cross making you my legate. You will then go as quickly as possible to the land of your people and announce the vilification and affliction suffered by our people and by this holy place. Rouse the hearts of the faithful to purify the holy sites in Jerusalem and to restore the offices of the saints! Through many dangers and temptations the gates of paradise are now opening for the chosen and the elect!"

Upon this marvelous revelation worthy of God, the vision faded, and Peter awakened from his dream. At first light of day he crossed the church's threshold, sought out the patriarch, outlined in order the details of the vision, and asked for a letter sealed with the holy cross endorsing his divine calling. The patriarch did not refuse but instead

[1] Simeon II was the Greek patriarch of Jerusalem from 1084 to 1099.

gratefully met his demands. License in hand, Peter returned to his homeland in accordance with his mission. Anxiously he boarded a ship to cross the sea and made landfall at the city of Bari. From there he hurried to Rome where he found the pope and described to him the mission that he had accepted from God and the patriarch, telling him also about the gentiles' impurities and about the sufferings of saints and pilgrims. The pope listened willingly and attentively and promised that he would obey in all things the commands and prayers of the saints.

19

THE ROSENFELD ANNALS

The Message of Peter the Hermit

Twelfth Century

A contemporary German monastic chronicle called The Rosenfeld Annals *gives more details about Peter's message. According to its author, Peter drew heavily upon an apocalyptic language similar to the prophecies of Pseudo-Methodius (see Document 9) and to the sermon that Guibert of Nogent imagined Urban II having preached (see Document 17).*

1096: In this year something never before seen or heard took place, presaged by frequent signs from heaven. Of these one shall be mentioned here in order to strengthen our faith in all the other signs. One evening, according to those who told about it, when there was not a cloud in the sky to cause it, lightning appeared to strike in various places around the globe, appearing again and again in different parts of the sky. It was concluded that this was not fire but angelic powers, which through their wandering signified a great movement, prefiguring the departure of people from their homes, which afterward happened throughout almost the entire Western world.

Annales Rosenveldenses, ed. G. H. Pertz, Monumenta Germaniae Historica, *Scriptores* 16 (Hannover: Hahnsche, 1849), 101–2. Translated by the author.

To make clear what these signs meant, a man named Peter came from the lands of Spain.[1] He was said first to have been a recluse there, but then to have left his cloister and through his preaching to have excited all of Provence—not just commoners but also kings, dukes, and other worldly leaders. Greater still, he persuaded bishops, monks, and other orders of the church to follow him. He carried with him a charter,[2] which he claimed had fallen to him from heaven and which commanded anyone in Christendom skilled at arms from whatever part of the world to pull up stakes and go to Jerusalem, there to do battle against the pagans and to take eternal possession of that city and its territories. To support all this he called upon the witness of the Gospel, where Jesus makes this pronouncement on the destruction of that city: *And Jerusalem will be downtrodden by peoples until the times of nations are fulfilled.*[3]

Everyone agreed to his words. Kingdoms were deprived of their rulers, cities of their pastors, villages of their residents. Not only men and boys but also many women took to this road.

[1] The Rosenfeld Annalist is unique in describing Peter as being from Spain.

[2] A charter, or *cartula*, was a medieval legal document usually used to record a transfer of property. This charter might be the letter from the patriarch of Jerusalem mentioned in Document 18.

[3] Luke 21:24.

20

Bohemond, a Norman Leader, Takes the Cross

ca. 1100

Among all the crusading princes, Bohemond of Taranto, the disinherited bastard son of a mercenary, had the least to lose by going to Jerusalem. What he lacked in financial resources he made up for in charisma and military cunning. The anonymous chronicle called The Deeds of the Franks, *compiled in the immediate aftermath of the crusade, describes the unusual circumstances that led Bohemond, in the midst of his family's wars for territorial conquest in southern Italy, to join the expedition to the Holy Land.*

The Deeds of the Franks and the Other Pilgrims to Jerusalem, ed. Rosalind Hill (London: T. Nelson, 1962), 7–8.

At that time the great warrior Bohemond was at the siege of Amalfi, at the Scafanti Bridge, when he heard that a countless number of Christian Franks were going to the Lord's Sepulcher and were preparing to do battle against a pagan people. He began carefully to ask what sorts of weapons these men bore, and what symbol of Christ they carried along the road, and what they shouted in battle. His questions were answered in order: "They carry suitable weapons for battle. They bear the cross of Christ on their right shoulder or else between their shoulders. They shout together in one voice thus: 'God wills it! God wills it!'"

Soon, moved by the Holy Spirit, he commanded that his most valuable cloak, which he was wearing, be cut up and straightaway had it turned into crosses. Then a great band of knights who had been at the siege ardently rushed to him. Soon Count Roger[1] alone remained at Amalfi, before returning in grief to Sicily and weeping because he had lost his followers. Then Lord Bohemond returned to his own land and scrupulously prepared himself to begin the road to the Holy Sepulcher.

[1] Roger of Sicily, Bohemond's uncle, in whose army Bohemond had been serving at Amalfi.

21

RALPH OF CAEN

Tancred Takes the Cross

ca. 1118

Tancred was Bohemond's nephew and appears to have acted as Bohemond's second-in-command while on crusade. As described by his biographer, the priest Ralph of Caen, who wrote around 1118, Tancred joined the campaign because of anxiety over the sins he had committed as a warrior and in hopes that this new type of warfare might help redeem his soul.

Ralph of Caen, *Gesta Tancredi*, in Recueil des Historiens des Croisades, *Historiens occidentaux* 3 (Paris: Imprimerie Royale, 1866), 605–6. Translated by the author.

Now I return to Tancred: The wealth of his family did not lead him to licentiousness, nor did the power of his relatives cause him pride. As an adolescent he excelled young men in his skill at arms, while surpassing old men in the seriousness of his behavior. Now to the former, now to the latter he presented a new demonstration of virtue. A careful student of God's commandments, he strove to listen to what he was told and to collect together what he had heard, and as much as his life among his peers allowed it, to carry out what he had learned. He deemed it wrong to disparage anyone, even when they disparaged him. Did not the one who heralded the mighty enemy's arrival say, "It is better for him to be slain than maligned"?[1] Tancred did not talk about himself at all, but he had an insatiable desire to be talked about. He preferred vigils to sleep, labor to rest, hunger to satiety, struggle to pleasure, the essential to the sumptuous.

Fame and glory alone moved his young mind. But the deeds that acquired honor for him also inflicted on him a deep and damaging wound. For he spared neither his own blood nor an enemy's. Turning these points over judiciously in his mind, he would burn with anxiety, for he understood that his military engagements contradicted the Lord's commands. The Lord orders that if one cheek is struck, the other is to be offered to the attacker, but the military life does not spare even family blood. The Lord admonishes us also to give a coat to one asking for a tunic, but military necessity urges that both these things and anything else beyond them must be taken as plunder. If a moment of rest were ever permitted to this wise man, the opposition between his two callings would sap him of his boldness.

But after Pope Urban's proclamation assigned remission of sins to any Christian who would fight against the gentiles, then the strength of the man was seemingly roused from its slumber, his power returned, his eyes opened, his bravery redoubled. Previously, as noted, his mind had been of two parts, uncertain which path to follow—the Gospel or the world? But now that his skill as a soldier turned to the service of Christ, the twofold reason for fighting enthused the man greater than you could believe. The supplies necessary for the journey were quickly prepared. Nor did that man collect great amounts of money, for he had made it his custom from boyhood to transfer wealth into the control of others before it fell into his own hands. He nevertheless supplied a soldier's arms, warhorses, mules, and other such things sufficient to the number of his cohort.

[1] See Psalms 55:11–12.

22

EKKEHARD OF AURA

Ekkehard of Aura on the Public Reaction to the Call to Crusade

ca. 1116

Ekkehard of Aura was a prolific historian and a pilgrim to Jerusalem in 1101. He is also one of the best sources for reaction on the ground to the call to liberate Jerusalem. As someone who was himself vulnerable to the appeal of pilgrimage to the Holy Land, Ekkehard's account of the buildup to crusade, probably written in around 1116, is especially valuable.

In the time of the Roman emperor Henry IV and of Alexius of Constantinople, according to the prediction of the Gospel, everywhere nation rose up against nation, and kingdom against kingdom, and there were great earthquakes in many places, plague and famine, terrors in the skies and other great portents. And since now the Gospel trumpet sounds the coming of the just judge to all people, behold![1] The universal church watches as the whole world reveals prophetic signs. At that time the Saracens possessed Jerusalem and had made it a servant to Babylon, the seat of the kingdom of Egypt; the Christian faith there was feeble, ransoming itself through daily tribute payments. Bethlehem, the house of the bread of angels,[2] was turned into a stable for pack animals, and all the churches around it had for many years been subject to the ridicule of pagans. . . .

In addition to the sign seen on the sun, which I have written about elsewhere, many other portents appeared in the skies and on the land, rousing no small number of formerly lethargic men to meet this challenge. I have chosen to insert a few of the most useful of these signs here, for to mention all of them would take too long. Around October 7,

[1] See Luke 21:5–10.
[2] That is, "the house of Christ."

Ekkehard of Aura, *Hierosolymita: De oppresione, liberatione ac restauratione Jerosolymitanae Ecclesiae*, in Recueil des Historiens des Croisades, *Historiens occidentaux* 5 (Paris: Imprimerie Royale, 1894), 12, 18–19. Translated by the author.

for example, I saw a comet holding its position in the southern skies, its scintillating light curving into the shape of a sword. The third year after this, on February 24, I observed another star in the east shifting its place, leaping back and forth over a great distance. Upon my oath I along with several witnesses also saw bloody clouds rising up from the west and the east and then crashing together in the middle of the sky. There also appeared in the middle of the night dazzling fires that floated through the air in the north like little torches.

One day a little before those years, in mid-afternoon, a priest of honorable life named Siggerius witnessed two horsemen charging through the skies and for a long time doing battle against one another. One of them held a cross of no small size with which he was seen victoriously to beat his opponent into submission. At the same time a priest named G, who now, as my fellow monk, has exchanged a lamb owed to Christ for a firstborn donkey,[3] was walking with two companions in the woods around midday. There he saw a sword of wondrous length that a whirlwind seemed to be waving about. How it had risen into the air in the first place he did not know, but eventually it flew so high that it disappeared, sounding a clangor that impressed the ears just as its metal had done the eyes. Others who were tending to horses in pastures tell how they saw an image of a city in the sky and that they could make out various crowds of people equally on horseback and on foot hastening along a road toward it.

A few people also revealed that the sign of the cross had been divinely stamped onto their clothing or their brow or some other body part and believed that by this stigmata they had been marked out for the army of the Lord. Similarly, others struck with a sudden change of heart or instructed in a night vision gave away their lands and worldly possessions and gladly had the sign of [the Lord's] death sewn onto their garments. All of these people formed unbelievably big crowds and rushed together to churches where priests, in a new rite, dispensed blessings to swords alongside staff and purse.[4] What shall I say about a woman at the time who had been pregnant for two straight years and whose womb finally opened and poured forth a talking baby? What about the infant born with twice the usual number of limbs, or another one with two heads, or all the lambs that issued forth with two heads, or the colts

[3] An esoteric reference to Exodus 13:13, implying simply that the priest had given up service in the world for service to Christ.

[4] The staff and purse are symbols of pilgrims, who normally traveled unarmed. Ekkehard thus comments on how revolutionary, if not self-contradictory, the idea of a crusader, an armed pilgrim, was.

born from mares who had really big teeth (commonly called "equines"), the likes of which you normally see on three-month-old packhorses?

Because of these signs and others like them, every creature joined his Creator's army, but the enemy—ever alert while others sleep—lost no time in raising up pseudo-prophets and mixing false brothers and deceitful people of either gender in the Lord's army, thus sowing his own chaff in the midst of that good seed. Through some hypocrisy and lies here, through other types of corruption there, he so infected the flocks of Christ that just as the good pastor foretold, even the elect were led into error.[5] Thus some concocted a fable that Charlemagne had risen from the dead to fight for this cause.[6] Something similar was said about another person (I don't know who) brought back to life. There was a story about a goose supposedly leading its lady to Jerusalem, and many others like this one. But these deceivers, wolves in sheep's clothing, were known and named through the fruits of their work—especially those among them who are still alive. One need only ask them at what port (according to their solemn word) they crossed the sea without a ship, at which places of battle with few companions they laid low many pagans, what weapons they carried there, at which section of Jerusalem's walls they set their camps, and so on. If they are unable to answer, they should be compelled to do penance for the offerings they hypocritically took from the faithful and for the crowds they abandoned for the sake of plunder, and especially for their apostasy.

[5] Matthew 2:24, where Christ identifies false prophets as a sign of the Last Days.

[6] The "King of the Romans and Greeks" in Pseudo-Methodius's prophecy (see Document 9) was sometimes thought to be a resurrected Charlemagne.

23

SOLOMON BEN SIMSON

The Massacre of the Jews of Mainz, Recounted in the Hebrew Chronicle

Mid-Twelfth Century

The first crusaders departed for the East in the spring of 1096. These early crusaders are mainly known for a series of massacres of Jews committed in cities along the Rhine River in Germany, recorded by both Christian and Jewish writers. The account excerpted here is usually attributed to Solomon ben Simson, a Jewish resident of Speyer who wrote in the mid-twelfth century. The leader of the anti-Jewish violence described in this selection was a man named Emicho of Flonheim. No doubt motivated in part by greed, Emicho was also a fanatic who tapped some of the ideas contained in the revelations of Pseudo-Methodius (see Document 9). The translation below is by Robert Chazan.

It came to pass on the new moon of Sivan[1] that Count Emicho, the persecutor of all the Jews—may his bones be ground up between millstones—came with a large army outside the city [of Mainz], with crusaders and common folk in tents. The gates of the city were locked before him. He also had said: "It is my desire to go on the crusade." He became head of the bands and concocted the story that an emissary of the Crucified had come to him and had given him a sign in his flesh indicating that, when he would reach Byzantium, then he [Jesus] would come to him [Emicho] himself and crown him with royal diadem and that he would overcome his enemies.[2] He was our chief persecutor. He

[1] May 25, 1096.

[2] The description calls to mind Pseudo-Methodius's prediction of a last "King of the Romans and Greeks," described in Document 9. The "sign in his flesh" is likely one of the apparent cross tattoos described by Ekkehard of Aura in Document 22.

---

had no mercy on the elderly or on the young women; he had no pity on the infant and the suckling and the sickly. He made the people of the Lord "like dust to be trampled." "Their young men he put to the sword and their pregnant women he ripped open." They camped outside the city for two days.

At the time when the wicked one came to Mainz on his way to Jerusalem, the elders of the people came to their archbishop, Ruthard, and bribed him with two hundred silver *zekukim*.[3] It had been his intention to go to the villages which belonged to the archbishops. But the [Jewish] community came, when they bribed him, and begged him, so that he stayed with them in Mainz. He brought all the community into his inner chambers and said: "I have wishes to remain here for your sakes, to assist you. You must therefore supply all our needs until the crusaders pass through." The [Jewish] community agreed to do so. The two—the archbishop and the burgrave[4]—agreed and said: "We shall either die with you or live with you." Then the community said: "Since those who are our neighbors and acquaintances have agreed to save us, let us also send to the wicked Emicho our moneys and our letters, so that the [Jewish] communities along the way will honor him. Perhaps the Lord will behave in accord with his great loving-kindness and will relent against us. For this purpose we have disbursed our moneys, giving the archbishop and his ministers and his servants and the burghers approximately four hundred silver *zekukim*." We gave the wicked Emicho seven gold pounds so that he might assist us. It was of no avail, and to this point no balm has been given for our affliction. For we were unlike Sodom and Gomorrah. For them ten [righteous] were sought in order to save them. For us neither twenty nor ten were sought.

It came to pass on the third day of Sivan,[5] which had been a day of sanctity and setting apart for Israel at the time of the giving of the Torah—on that day when Moses our teacher, may his memory be blessed, said: "Be ready for the third day"[6]—on that day the [Jewish] community of Mainz, the pious of the Almighty, were set apart in holiness and purity and were sanctified to ascend to God all together. "Cherished in life, in death they were not parted."[7] For all of them were in the courtyard of the archbishop. . . .

[3] The value of two hundred *zekukim* is uncertain. It was, however, the amount of the dowry, or bride-price, owed to a bride if for any reason her marriage should end.

[4] Count.

[5] May 27, 1096.

[6] Exodus 9:11.

[7] 2 Samuel 1:23.

It came to pass at midday that the wicked Emicho, persecutor of the Jews, came—he and all his army—to the gate. The burghers opened the gate to him. Then the enemies of the Lord said to one another: "Behold the gate has been opened before us. Now let us avenge the blood of the Crucified." When the children of the holy covenant—the saintly ones, the God-fearing—who were there saw the huge multitude, the army as large "as the sand on the seashore," they cleaved to their Creator. They donned armor and strapped on weapons—great and small—with R. Kalonymous ben R. Meshullam the *parnas*[8] at their head. But from their great anguish and from the many fasts undertaken, they did not have sufficient strength to stand up before the enemy. They then came in battalions and companies, sweeping down like a river, until Mainz was filled completely. The enemy Emicho made an announcement to the citizenry that they surrender and remove the enemy [the Jews] from the city. "A great panic from the Lord fell upon them."[9] The men of Israel strapped on their weapons in the innermost courtyard of the archbishop and all of them approached the gate [of the courtyard] to do battle with the crusaders and the burghers. They did battle against one another at the gate. Our sins brought it about that the enemy overcame them and captured the gate. "The hand of the Lord lay heavy" upon his people. Then all the gentiles gathered against the Jews in the courtyard, in order to destroy them totally. The hands of our people wavered, when they saw the hand of wicked Edom had overcome them.[10] Indeed the men of the archbishop himself fled from his church, for they intended to kill him as well, since he had spoken up on behalf of Israel.

The enemy entered the courtyard on the third of Sivan, on the third day of the week, "a day of darkness and gloom, a day of densest clouds." "May darkness and day gloom reclaim it"; "may God above have no concern for it; may light never shine upon it." Woe for the day when we saw the anguish of our souls. Stars, why did you not cover your light—was not Israel compared to the stars? The twelve constellations, like the number of the tribes of Jacob, why did you not extinguish your light from shining on the enemy that intended to blot out the name of Israel?

When the children of the sacred covenant saw that the decree had been enacted and that the enemy had overcome them, they entered the courtyard and all cried out together—elders, young men and young women, children, menservants and maidservants—to their Father in

[8] The chief administrative officer of a Jewish congregation.

[9] Zechariah 14:13.

[10] The Edomites in the Bible are enemies of David. In medieval Jewish intellectual tradition, they represented Rome.

heaven. They wept for themselves and their lives. They accepted upon themselves the judgment of heaven. They said to one another: "Let us be strong and suffer the yoke of the sacred awe. For the moment the enemy will kill us, but the easiest of the four deaths is by the sword. We shall, however, remain alive; our souls [shall be] in paradise, in the radiance of the great light forever." They said unreservedly and willingly: "Ultimately, one must not question the ways of the Holy One, blessed be he and blessed be his Name, who gave us his Torah and the commandment to put to death and to kill ourselves for the unity of his holy Name. . . ." ". . . Anyone who has a knife should inspect it, that it not be defective. Then he should come and slaughter us for the sanctification of the unique [God] who lives forever. Subsequently he should slaughter himself by his throat or should thrust the knife into his belly.["]

The enemy, immediately upon entering the courtyard, found there some of the perfectly pious with Rabbi Isaac ben R. Moses the dialectician. He stretched out his neck and they cut off his head immediately. They had clothed themselves in their fringed garments and had seated themselves in the midst of the courtyard in order to do speedily the will of their Creator. They did not wish to flee to the chambers in order to go on living briefly. Rather, with love they accepted upon themselves the judgment of heaven. The enemy rained stones and arrows upon them, but they did not deign to flee. They struck down all those whom they found there, with "blows of sword, death, and destruction." . . .

. . . The pious women, the daughters of kings threw coins and silver out the windows at the enemy, so that they be occupied with gathering the money, in order to impede them slightly until they might finish slaughtering their sons and daughters. The hands of merciful mothers slaughtered their children, in order to do the will of their Creator.

When the enemy came to the chambers and broke down the doors and found them still convulsing and writhing in blood, they took their money and stripped them naked and smote those who remained. They did not leave "a remnant or a residue." Thus they did in all the chambers where the children of the holy covenant were, with the exception of one chamber that was somewhat stronger. The enemy did battle against them till evening. When the saintly ones saw that the enemy was stronger than they and that they would be unable to withstand them any longer, they bestirred themselves and rose up—men and women—and slaughtered the children first. Subsequently the saintly women threw stones through the windows against the enemy. The enemy threw stones against them. They took the stones until their flesh and faces became shredded. They cursed and blasphemed the crusaders in the name of the Crucified, the impure and foul, the son of lust: "Upon whom do you trust? Upon a rotting corpse!" The crusaders advanced to break down the door.

"Who has seen anything like this; who has heard anything" like that which the saintly and pious woman, Rachel daughter of R. Isaac ben R. Asher, wife of R. Judah, did? She said to her companions: "I have four children. On them as well have no mercy, lest these uncircumcised come and seize them alive and they remain in their pseudofaith. With them as well you must sanctify the Name of the holy God." One of her companions came and took the knife to slaughter her son. When the mother of the children saw the knife, she shouted loudly and bitterly and smote her face and breast and said: "Where is your steadfast love, O Lord?" Then the woman said to her companions in her bitterness: "Do not slaughter Isaac before his brother Aaron, so that he not see the death of his brother and take flight." The woman took the lad and slaughtered him—he was small and exceedingly comely. The mother spread her sleeve to receive the blood; she received the blood in her sleeves instead of in the [Temple] vessel for blood. The lad Aaron, when he saw that his brother had been slaughtered, cried out: "Mother, do not slaughter me!" He went and hid under a bureau. She still had two daughters, Bella and Matrona, comely and beautiful young women, the daughters of R. Judah her husband. The girls took the knife and sharpened it, so that it not be defective. They stretched forth their necks and she sacrificed them to the Lord God of Hosts, who commanded us not to renounce pure awe of him and to remain faithful to him, as it is written: "You must be wholehearted with the Lord your God."[11] When the saintly one completed sacrificing her three children before the Creator, then she raised her voice and called to her son: "Aaron, Aaron, where are you? I shall not have mercy nor pity on you as well." She pulled him by the leg from under the bureau where he was hidden and she sacrificed him before the sublime and exalted God. She placed them under her two sleeves, two on each side, near her heart. They convulsed near her, until the enemy seized the chamber and found her sitting and mourning them. They said to her: "Show us the moneys which you have in your sleeves." When they saw the children and saw that they were slaughtered, they smote and killed her along with them. . . .

After the children of the holy covenant who were in the [archbishop's] chambers were killed, the crusaders came upon them, to strip the corpses and to remove them from the chambers. They threw them naked to the ground through the windows—heap upon heap, mound

[11] Deuteronomy 18:13.

upon mound, until they formed a high heap. Many were still alive as they threw them. Their souls were still attached to their bodies and they still had a bit of life. They signaled to them with their fingers: "Give us a bit of water that we might drink." When the crusaders saw them, that there was still life in them, they asked them: "Do you wish to sully yourselves?[12] Then we shall give you water to drink and you will still be able to be saved." They shook their heads and looked to their Father in heaven, saying, "No." They pointed with their fingers to the Holy One blessed be he, but could not utter a word from their mouths as a result of the many wounds which had been inflicted upon them. They continued to smite them mightily, beyond those [earlier] blows, until they killed them a second time.

[12] That is to say, "Will you agree to be baptized?"

4
The Crusade and Constantinople

24

ANNA COMNENA

Anna Comnena Describes Peter the Hermit's Crusade

ca. 1148

Emicho of Flonheim never reached Jerusalem. His followers instead engaged the king of Hungary on the borders of his realm and suffered a near-total defeat. The few survivors either returned home or joined other crusading armies departing from Italy. Some of the early crusaders, however, did make it as far as Constantinople, including the contingent led by Peter the Hermit. Anna Comnena, the daughter of the emperor Alexius, wrote an account of the pilgrims' eventual fate in the context of a biography of her father. The text was composed about fifty years after the events she describes here but seems to preserve something akin to accepted historical memory of the crusade at Alexius's court.

The emperor knew what Peter had suffered before from the Turks and advised him to wait for the other counts to arrive, but he refused, confident in the number of his followers. He crossed the Sea of Marmora and pitched camp near a small place called Helenopolis.[1] Later, some

[1] In doing so, Peter's armies were settling on the frontier lands between Byzantium and the territory recently captured by the Seljuk Turks.

Anna Comnena, *The Alexiad*, trans. E. R. A. Sewter (London: Penguin Books, 1969), 311–13.

Normans, 10,000 in all, joined him but detached themselves from the rest of the army and ravaged the outskirts of Nicaea, acting with horrible cruelty to the whole population; they cut in pieces some of the babies, impaled others on wooden spits and roasted them over a fire; old people were subjected to every kind of torture. The inhabitants of the city, when they learnt what was happening, threw open their gates and charged out against them. A fierce battle ensued, in which the Normans fought with such spirit that the Nicaeans had to retire inside their citadel. The enemy therefore returned to Helenopolis with all the booty. There an argument started between them and the rest (who had not gone on the raid)—the usual quarrel in such cases—for the latter were green with envy. That led to brawling, whereupon the daredevil Normans broke away for a second time and took Xerigordos by assault.[2] The sultan's reaction was to send Elkhanes with a strong force to deal with them.[3] He arrived at Xerigordos and captured it; of the Normans some were put to the sword and others taken prisoner. At the same time Elkhanes made plans to deal with the remainder, still with Koukoupetros.[4] He laid ambushes in suitable places, hoping that the enemy on their way to Nicaea would fall into the trap unawares and be killed. Knowing the Keltic love of money he also enlisted the services of two determined men who were to go to Peter's camp and there announce that the Normans, having seized Nicaea, were sharing out all the spoils of the city. This story had an amazing effect on Peter's men; they were thrown into confusion at the words "share" and "money"; without a moment's hesitation they set out on the Nicaea road in complete disorder, practically heedless of military discipline and the proper arrangement which should mark men going off to war. As I have said before, the Latin race at all times is unusually greedy for wealth, but when it plans to invade a country, neither reason nor force can restrain it. They set out helter-skelter, regardless of their individual companies. Near the Drakon they fell into the Turkish ambuscade and were miserably slaughtered. So great a multitude of Kelts and Normans died by the Ishmaelite sword that when they gathered the remains of the fallen, lying on every side, they heaped up, I will not say a mighty ridge or hill or peak, but a mountain of considerable height and depth and width, so huge was the mass of bones. Some men of the same race as the

[2] A fortress held by the Turks of Nicaea.

[3] The sultan is Kilij Arslan I, who from 1092 to 1107 ruled the Seljuk sultanate of Rum (the Turkish name for Rome), created out of territories captured from Byzantium. Elkhanes was one of his generals.

[4] Peter the Hermit.

slaughtered barbarians later, when they were building a wall like those of a city, used the bones of the dead as pebbles to fill up the cracks. In this way the city became their tomb. To this very day it stands with its encircling wall built of mixed stones and bones. When the killing was over, only Peter with a handful of men returned to Helenopolis. The Turks, wishing to capture him, again laid an ambush, but the emperor, who had heard of this and indeed of the terrible massacre, thought it would be an awful thing if Peter also became a prisoner.[5] Constantine Euphorbenus Catacalon (already mentioned often in this history)[6] was accordingly sent with powerful contingents in warships across the straits to help him. At his approach the Turks took to their heels. Without delay Catacalon picked up Peter and his companions (there were only a few) and brought them in safety to Alexius, who reminded Peter of his foolishness in the beginning and added that these great misfortunes had come upon him through not listening to his advice. With the usual Latin arrogance Peter disclaimed responsibility and blamed his men for them, because (said he) they had been disobedient and followed their own whims. He called them brigands and robbers, considered unworthy therefore by the Saviour to worship at His Holy Sepulchre.

[5] According to Latin sources, Peter was in fact in Constantinople negotiating with Alexius at the time the Turks attacked his followers.

[6] Anna had mentioned Catacalon twice before in the history, describing him as one of the leading citizens to whom Alexius frequently entrusted military missions.

25

The Crusaders at Constantinople: A Latin Perspective

ca. 1100

The crusader princes took different paths, but all of them, like Peter the Hermit's armies, passed through Constantinople. Here the writer of The Deeds of the Franks *describes the early stages of the expedition of Bohemond, whose army he seems to have accompanied. The anonymous author emphasizes the growing tensions between the Latin and Greek*

The Deeds of the Franks and the Other Pilgrims to Jerusalem, ed. Rosalind Hill (London: T. Nelson, 1962), 10–13. Translated by the author.

Christians as they approached the Byzantine capital, while inside the city Emperor Alexius tried to combine Greek diplomacy and Latin customary oaths to assert his own control over the army.

The dreadful emperor sent to our men one of his messengers whom he held especially dear and whom they call a *kyriopalatios*,[1] so that he might lead us safely through his land until we reached Constantinople. And when we passed by those cities, he ordered the residents of the land to open markets for us, just as those whom I mentioned earlier had done.[2] To be sure they feared Lord Bohemond's powerful people so much that they did not allow any of us actually to enter their cities. Our men wished to attack and seize one of the castles, because it was filled with supplies, but the wise man Bohemond did not agree, not wishing to treat the land unjustly or to break faith with the emperor. For this reason he grew angry at Tancred and certain others. That was in the evening.

The next morning, the residents of the castle came outside, and carrying crosses in their hands, they formed a procession and approached Bohemond. He received them gladly and happily permitted them to depart. Then we came to a city called Serres, where we fixed our tents and had a market with enough supplies for the time being. There Bohemond struck an agreement with two *kyriopalatioi*, and in return for their friendship he ordered our men to treat the land justly and to return all the animals seized as plunder.

Then we arrived at the city of Rusa. The Greeks came out and joyfully entered into the presence of Lord Bohemond, setting before us a huge market. And there we pitched our tents on the fourth day before Easter;[3] there also Bohemond left all his people behind and set forth to speak with the emperor at Constantinople, taking with him a few soldiers. Tancred stayed behind as head of the army of Christ, and seeing the pilgrims buying food, he decided to leave the road and take his people where they might live easily. Then he went down into a valley full of all kinds of goods suitable to nourish a body. There we devotedly observed Easter.

When the emperor had heard that that most esteemed of men Bohemond had come to him, he commanded that he be worthily received and

[1] Meaning "Lord of the Palace."

[2] The author is referring to the relatively warm reception the army had received in Macedonia. As the Franks marched farther into Byzantium, their relations with the locals grew ever more tense.

[3] April 1, 1097.

carefully lodged him outside the city. Having lodged him, the emperor sent for him to come and speak secretly with him. Then there came there Duke Godfrey with his brother; and then the count of Saint-Gilles neared the city.[4] Then the emperor, troubled and simmering with rage, thought cunningly and deceitfully about how he might rein in these warriors of Christ. But by the intervention of God's grace, neither he nor his men found a time or place to harm them. All the more nobly born princes of Constantinople had recently assembled out of fear that they might lose their homeland, and they decided through counsel and cunning schemes that our dukes, counts, and great men should faithfully make an oath to the emperor. Our men protested vigorously, saying: "Surely it would be unworthy of us and altogether unjust to make an oath to him!"

Perhaps henceforth our leaders would often mislead us. What did they do in the end? They will say that they humbled themselves according to the will of the most wicked emperor due to necessity, whether they wanted it or not. But to the bravest of men, Bohemond, whom the emperor greatly feared, since he had often driven him from the field with his army, Alexius said that if he, Bohemond, freely made an oath to him, he would give him lands a fifteen-day journey in length and an eight-day journey in breadth around Antioch. The emperor further pledged to Bohemond that if he faithfully kept this oath, then he would not break his own either. Such brave and strong men—why did they do this? They did it because necessity compelled them.

The emperor pledged faith and security to all of our men and promised that he would also accompany them with an army through land and sea, and that he would steadfastly provide us with a market on land and sea, and that he would carefully recompense us for all our losses, concluding that he did not wish and would not allow any of our pilgrims to be disturbed or troubled while on the road.

The count of Saint-Gilles, however, had been lodged in a suburb outside the city, and his people stayed behind. The emperor ordered the count to make homage and fealty to him just as the others had done, and while the emperor ordered these things, the count thought about how

[4] Godfrey had arrived at Constantinople in December 1096. Bohemond reached the city around April 10, 1097. Raymond of Saint-Gilles appeared there around April 21. The chronology in this passage is confused, indicating either that the text is corrupt or that, because of the secretive character of these negotiations, the author simply did not know exactly what had happened.

he might take vengeance on the imperial army. But Duke Godfrey and Count Robert of Flanders and other princes said to him that it wouldn't be just to fight against Christians. The wise man Bohemond said that if he did anything unjust to the emperor, that he would take the emperor's part. The count therefore took counsel with his men and pledged life and honor to Alexius, that he would neither harm him nor agree to allow another to harm him. When asked about homage, he said that he would not do it at the risk of losing his head. Then the people of Lord Bohemond approached Constantinople.

26

An Eleventh-Century Mosaic Depicting a Byzantine, Imperial Christ

Eleventh Century

In this mosaic, Christ is depicted in imperial robes and seated between a Greek emperor and his wife, inside the grand church of the Hagia Sophia in Constantinople (modern Istanbul).

ΑΥΤΟΚΡΑΤΩΡ ΠΙCΤΟC
ΒΑCΙΛΕΥC ΡΩΜΑΙΩΝ
ΙC
ΧC
ΒΕCΤΑΤΗ
ΑΥΓΟΥCΤΑ

27

ANNA COMNENA

Anna Comnena Describes the Crusaders at Constantinople

ca. 1148

Unsurprisingly, Anna Comnena had a very different perspective from The Deeds of the Franks. *Her account gives some insight into Byzantine diplomatic rituals, which Alexius and Bohemond each tried to manipulate to the other's detriment. Anna indicates that her father got the better of the Norman warrior, who had made war against Alexius before the crusade and would do so again afterward. Her pro-Byzantine perspective does not by itself impugn her testimony, though her analysis ought to be carefully compared with that in Document 25.*

When Bohemond came into his presence, Alexius at once gave him a smile and inquired about his journey. Where had he left the counts? Bohemond replied frankly and to the best of his knowledge to all these questions, while the emperor politely reminded him of his daring deeds at Larissa and Dyrrachium; he also recalled Bohemond's former hostility.[1] "I was indeed an enemy and foe then," said Bohemond, "but now I come of my own free will as Your Majesty's friend." Alexius talked at length with him, in a somewhat discreet way trying to discover the man's real feelings, and when he concluded that Bohemond would be prepared to take the oath of allegiance, he said to him, "You are tired now from your journey. Go away and rest. Tomorrow we can discuss matters of common interest." Bohemond went off to the Cosmidion,[2] where an apartment had been made ready for him and a rich table was laid full of delicacies and food of all kinds. Later the cooks brought in meat and flesh of animals and birds, uncooked. "The food, as you see,

[1] Bohemond fought alongside his father, Robert Guiscard, in wars against Alexius during the years 1080–1085, often leading the armies himself.

[2] A monastery placed just outside the walls of Constantinople.

Anna Comnena, *The Alexiad*, trans. E. R. A. Sewter (London: Penguin Books, 1969), 326–30.

has been prepared by us in our customary way," they said, "but if that does not suit you here is raw meat which can be cooked in whatever way you like." In doing so and saying this they were carrying out the emperor's instructions. Alexius was a shrewd judge of a man's character, cleverly reading the innermost thoughts of his heart, and knowing the spiteful, malevolent nature of Bohemond, he rightly guessed what would happen. It was in order that Bohemond might have no suspicions that he caused the uncooked meat to be set before him at the same time, and it was an excellent move. The cunning Frank not only refused to taste any of the food, but would not even touch it with his finger-tips; he rejected it outright, but divided it all up among the attendants, without a hint of his own secret misgivings. It looked as if he was doing them a favour, but that was mere pretence: in reality, if one considers the matter rightly, he was mixing them a cup of death. There was no attempt to hide his treachery, for it was his habit to treat servants with utter indifference. However, he told his own cooks to prepare the raw meat in the usual Frankish way. On the next day he asked the attendants how they felt. "Very well," they replied, and added that they had suffered not the slightest harm from it. At these words he revealed his hidden fear: "For my own part," he said, "when I remembered the wars I have fought with him, not to mention the famous battle, I was afraid he might arrange to kill me by putting a dose of poison in the food." Such were the actions of Bohemond. I must say I have never seen an evil man who in all his deeds and words did not depart from the path of right; whenever a man leaves the middle course, to whatever extreme he inclines he takes his stand far from virtue. Bohemond was summoned then and required, like the others, to take the customary Latin oath. Knowing what his position was he acquiesced gladly enough, for he had neither illustrious ancestors nor great wealth (hence his forces were not strong—only a moderate number of Keltic followers). In any case, Bohemond was by nature a liar. . . .

[At a later meeting with Bohemond and other leaders, Alexius offered advice about the battles to come.]

After a conversation with the Franks and after showing his friendship for them with all kinds of presents and honours, on the next day [Alexius] took his seat on the imperial throne. Bohemond and the others were sent for and warned about the things likely to happen on their journey. He gave them profitable advice. They were instructed in the methods normally used by the Turks in battle; told how they should draw up a battle-line, how to lay ambushes; advised not to pursue far when the enemy ran away in flight. In this way, by means of money and good advice, he did much to soften their ferocious nature. Then he proposed that they should cross the straits. For one of them, Raymond the Count of Saint-Gilles, Alexius had a deep affection, for several reasons: the count's superior intellect, his untarnished reputation, the purity of his life. He knew moreover how greatly Raymond valued the truth: whatever the circumstances, he honoured truth above all else. In fact, Saint-Gilles outshone all Latins in every quality, as the sun is brighter than the stars. It was for this that Alexius detained him for some time. Thus, when all the others had taken their leave of him and made the journey across the straits of the Propontis to Damalion, and when he was now relieved of their troublesome presence, he sent for him on many occasions. He explained in more detail the adventures that the Latins must expect to meet with on their march; he also laid bare his own suspicions of their plans. In the course of many conversations on this subject he unreservedly opened the doors of his soul, as it were, to the count; he warned him always to be on his guard against Bohemond's perfidy, so that if attempts were made to break the treaty he might frustrate them and in every way thwart Bohemond's schemes. Saint-Gilles pointed out that Bohemond inherited perjury and guile from his ancestors—it was a kind of heirloom. "It will be a miracle if he keeps his sworn word," he said. "As far as I am concerned, however, I will always try to the best of my ability to observe your commands." With that he took his leave of the emperor and went off to join the whole Keltic army. Alexius would have liked to share in the expedition against the barbarians, too, but he feared the enormous numbers of the Kelts. He did think it wise, though, to move to Pelekanum. Making his permanent headquarters near Nicaea, he could obtain information about their progress and at the same time about Turkish activities outside the city, as well as about the condition of the inhabitants inside. It would be shameful, he believed, if in the meantime he did not himself win some military success. When a favourable opportunity arose, he planned to capture Nicaea himself; that would be preferable to receiving it from the Kelts (according to the agreement already made with them). Nevertheless, he kept the idea to himself.

28

COUNT STEPHEN OF BLOIS

From Constantinople to Nicaea: A Letter from Count Stephen of Blois

June 24, 1097

The first great battle of the crusade was the siege of Nicaea, whose details Count Stephen of Blois describes in a letter to his wife, Adele, written on June 24, 1097, just five days after the siege had ended. Stephen was one of the leaders of the last of the Frankish contingents to reach Constantinople, and hence the last to arrive at Nicaea.

Count Stephen sends to Countess Adele, his wife and sweetest friend, all his mind's good and kindly thoughts.

Let it be known to you, my sweet, that I am honored and well rested while on the blessed road, and that from the shores of Constantinople I have already taken care to send you news about my life and pilgrimage. But in case some accident befalls that legate, I am writing a letter to you again. With God's help I joyfully arrived at the city of Constantinople. The emperor received me worthily, honorably, and affectionately—as if I were his son—and gave me many valuable gifts. In the whole army of God and in ours there was not duke or count or any other powerful person in whom he invested more faith or showed more affection than me. Truly, my dear, his imperial dignity urged us and advised us to entrust one of our sons to him. He promised to bestow such great and splendid honors on him that he would have little reason to envy me.[1] I tell you truthfully that there is no man under the heavens like him today. He has generously enriched all our leaders, he has given gifts to every knight, and he has refreshed all of the poor with great meals. Near Nicaea there is a fortification called Civitot, near to which is the Bosporus, through

[1] Sons anxious for their inheritance were known to rebel against their fathers, a possibility to which Stephen here appears to allude.

Heinrich Hagenmeyer, *Die Kreuzzugsbriefe aus den Jahren 1088–1100* (Hildesheim: Georg Olms, 1901), ep. 4, 138–40. Translated by the author.

which the pious emperor's own ships travel day and night. They bring food to the numberless poor and distribute it to them daily. In our days, it seems to me, there has not been a prince so distinguished and honorable in every aspect of his character. Your father,[2] my sweet, performed many great acts of charity, but they are as nothing compared to this man. I have written these few things about him to you so that you might know what sort of person he is.

After ten days of him showing me such respect, I left him, as if a father. He ordered ships prepared for me so that I might swiftly cross the tranquil Bosporus, which surrounds that city. Some have described that sea crossing as savage and dangerous, but their words are false. For it is no less uncertain than is the Marne or the Seine. Then we came to another channel called "the Arm of St. George," which we crossed in stages since we were not able to find an overabundance of ships. We then directed our course to the city of Nicomedia, laid low by the Turks, where the aforesaid channel reaches its head and its end. There the blessed martyr Pantaleon suffered for Christ.[3] Then we hurried to the great city of Nicaea, praising God as we went.

Nicaea, my beloved, is surrounded by wondrous walls and by more than three hundred tall towers. We found it full of bold Turkish fighters, and we learned that the numberless army of God for four weeks had experienced there against the Nicaeans death-dealing combat. Suleiman, the prince of the Turks, ready for battle and at the head of a great host, had come upon the army a little before us, and suddenly attacked our men.[4] He believed that this fast charge would allow him to break into the city and aid his people. By God's mercy his wicked plan went other than intended. Our men prepared quickly and with brave souls welcomed the Turks, who immediately turned tail and gave themselves over to flight.[5] Our men gave fierce pursuit and killed many of them. Hounding them over a great distance, they killed some, wounded others, and had it not been for the steep and unfamiliar mountains, they would have suffered a great and irreparable loss. None of our men died, but afterward our great army together made many ferocious assaults with bow and ballista and killed many Turks, including some of their leaders. Some of our men were killed, but truly not many. The only knight of any fame to die was Baldwin of Flanders, Count of Ghent.

[2] William the Conqueror, Duke of Normandy and king of England.

[3] Martyred during the Diocletian persecution in 303.

[4] The leader of the Turks was Kilij Arslan, the sultan of Rum. His father was Suleiman.

[5] The unexpected arrival of Raymond of Saint-Gilles and his army played a crucial role in the Franks' victory.

Eventually our godly princes realized that Nicaea was so well fortified, as I have said, that it couldn't be conquered with weapons. Laboriously, they erected tall wooden towers with sturdy walls and various sorts of weapons. The Turks saw all this. Fearful, they sent messengers to the emperor and surrendered the city, on one condition: that they be given safe conduct to leave the city unarmed and be handed over in chains but alive to the emperor.[6] Upon hearing these terms, the esteemed emperor came to us. He was not anxious to enter into his own city of Nicaea, lest the crowds of people who venerated him as a pious father should crush him during the celebrations. Instead he withdrew to a nearby island on the sea to which all our princes (except for the Count of Saint-Gilles and me) hurriedly assembled so that they might celebrate their victory with him. When he heard that I had stayed at the city, lest another band of Turks come to its benefit and to the detriment of our army, he was most grateful. Nobly and happily he took the news that I had stayed behind as if I had given him a mountain of gold. From the island where he was staying, the great emperor arranged the more valuable of the spoils from the city of Nicaea so that the knights might have gold, silver, gemstones, textiles, horses, and things of this sort. All the food he distributed to the foot soldiers. As for the princes, he contrived to enrich them from his own treasures.

As I have said, thanks to our conquering God the great city of Nicaea was handed over on June 19. We read how in the early church the Holy Fathers celebrated a sacred council at Nicaea, and there the Arian heresy was demolished and through the instruction of the Holy Spirit, belief in the Trinity confirmed.[7] Afterward, because of sin, the rule of error[8] was established in that city, but now, with God's help, through his sinful servants, she has again become a disciple of truth. I tell you, my sweet, that from this oft-mentioned Nicaea we should arrive at Jerusalem in just five weeks, unless Antioch should slow us down.

Farewell!

[6] Stephen curiously leaves out the key military detail: that the emperor and the crusaders transported ships overland and put them on the Ascanian Lake, next to Nicaea, thus completing the blockade of the city on both land and water.

[7] The Council of Nicaea, held in 325.

[8] By this phrase, Stephen refers to Islam.

29

FULCHER OF CHARTRES

Fulcher of Chartres on the Battle of Dorylaeum

ca. 1106

Less than two weeks after the fall of Nicaea, its now deposed emir, Kilij Arslan, led a large cavalry contingent against the crusading army, which had divided itself in half. Bohemond of Taranto was leading the troops who first engaged the Turks. The other part of the army, led by Raymond of Saint-Gilles and Godfrey of Bouillon, was several miles away, following a slightly different route to Antioch. The priest, chronicler, and crusader Fulcher of Chartres—who seems to have written the first draft of his chronicle around the year 1101—was traveling with Bohemond and found himself caught up in the chaos of the battle, fought near the city of Dorylaeum.

When our barons had received permission from the emperor to depart, we set out from Nicaea on June 28 heading into the heartland of Romania.[1] But after we had traveled two days, we heard that the Turks had set a trap for us on the plain that we were going to cross, expecting to engage us in battle. After hearing this news, however, we lost none of our boldness. That evening many of our scouts observed them from a distance and warned us, causing us to set guards all around our tents to keep watch through the night. On the morning of July 1, however, we set forth in order, arms taken up, standards raised, horns sounding warning, cohorts established on the wings, with tributes and centurions appropriately leading the centuries.[2]

Then, at the second hour of the day, their advance guard came upon our scouts. Upon hearing this, we pitched our tents next to a marsh

[1] Romania here refers to Anatolia, roughly equivalent to modern Turkey, over which the Byzantine Empire claimed control.

[2] Fulcher draws heavily on an ancient Roman military vocabulary to describe the disposition of the crusading armies.

Fulcher of Chartres, *Historia Hierosolymitana*, ed. Heinrich Hagenmeyer (Heidelberg: Carl Winter, 1913), 189–99. Translated by the author.

so that we might set aside our packs and be ready for battle. And now look at the Turks! Following their emir and leader, Suleiman, who had held the city of Nicaea and Romania in his power, the Turks and pagan Persians at his command had gathered together from a distance of thirty days or more of travel. Numerous princes and emirs accompanied them, including Admircaradigum, Miriathos, and many others. All together they were estimated to number 360,000 warriors, which is to say archers.[3] Their custom is to rely on that weapon. All of them ride horses. By comparison, we had foot soldiers and horsemen. At that moment we also were missing Duke Godfrey, Count Raymond, and Hugh the Great. Two days before, I don't know why, they followed a different path at a crossroads, taking with them a great number of people. Because of this we suffered an incomparable loss. Many of ours died while the Turks were neither killed nor restrained. Our messengers were late reaching the rest of the army, and thus they were late coming to our rescue.

The Turks meanwhile were screaming and shouting and viciously raining down arrows upon us. We were dumbfounded and near death. Many were wounded, and we turned our backs and ran. This flight is not as remarkable as it sounds, since none of us had experienced a battle like this one.

And now thick crowds of them on the other side of the marsh forcefully charged our tents and entered them and began to plunder our goods and kill our people. With God's help, however, an advance guard from Hugh the Great and Count Raymond and Duke Godfrey rushed upon this disaster from the rear of the camp, and because we at the same time were fleeing into our tents, the Turks who had entered them immediately went back outside. They believed that we were running into the tents to fight them, but what they took for courage and wisdom, had they known it, was really just terror.

What more can I say? All of us crowded together as one, like lambs in a sheepfold, trembling and terrified by the enemies surrounding us on all sides such that we could not safely move in any direction. This was happening, we realized, because of our sins; some of us had been corrupted by extravagance and avarice, and various other types of wickedness had befouled others still. Men, women, and children raised to heaven feverish shouts, mixed in with the cries of the pagans who were falling upon us. Now we had no hope of survival. We confessed our-

[3] Fulcher exaggerates the number of Turks. The high number, like the exotically named emirs, are intended to communicate a sense of wonder and fear to Latin readers.

selves guilty sinners and devotedly sought God's mercy. Our patron, the bishop of Le Puy, was there along with four other bishops.[4] Numerous priests were there as well, clad in white vestments, humbly beseeching the Lord to lay low our enemies' strength and shower us with gifts of his mercy. They sang and cried, they cried and sang. Then many rushed to the priests and afraid of death quickly confessed their sins to them. Meanwhile our leaders, Count Robert of Normandy, Count Stephen of Blois, Count Robert of Flanders, and Bohemond fought back to the best of their abilities and attempted to wade into the Turks, who in turn fought back manfully.

But perhaps our pleadings appeased the Lord, since he does not grant victory to arrogant nobles or splendid arms but instead in times of need dutifully comes to the aid of pure minds steeped in divine virtues. Thus he restored a little energy to us and more and more weakened the Turks, who now saw our comrades who were rushing in from the rear of the camp to help us. We praised God as our courage returned and rushed out in crowds and cohorts fighting to resist them. But alas! How many of our men who had been limping along at the rear of the army died on the road! From the first to the sixth hour of the day we were trapped in narrow straits, but then revivified little by little and strengthened by our friends, we felt the miracle of heavenly grace. In an instant, it seemed, all the Turks had turned their backs and fled!

We pursued them through mountains and valleys shouting at them ferociously and did not cease to chase them until our men in the front lines reached their tents. Some of us loaded down many camels and horses with things gathered from the Turks' tents and possessions, abandoned there out of fear; others pursued the fleeing Turks until nightfall. It was a great miracle of God that on the second and third day they did not cease to run, even though no one except God was pursuing them. We rejoiced over such a victory, giving all praise to God, who did not wish our journey to be brought to such an ending, but rather wished it to prosper more nobly than usual and to the ennoblement of Christian practice. The tale of this victory shall forever resound from Orient to Occident.

[4] Bishop Adhémar of Le Puy in fact would have been accompanying Count Raymond with the other army and could not have been present in the tent with Fulcher.

30

RAYMOND OF AGUILERS

Raymond of Aguilers on the Battle of Dorylaeum

ca. 1100

The priest Raymond of Aguilers was with the other half of the crusade host and thus describes the battle from the perspective of the men who rushed to Bohemond's rescue. Like Fulcher of Chartres (see Document 29), Raymond seeks to explain the apparently miraculous character of the Franks' victory.

We set forth from the city of Nicaea into Romania, where on the second day Bohemond and other princes heedlessly broke away from the count and bishop and duke.[1] On the third day of this separation as he ordered their camps set, his men saw 150,000 Turks approaching and ready for combat. He organized his men and made battle arrangements as time allowed but lost many of the soldiers who had followed him. In the midst of all this he sent word to the count and duke, who were two miles away, to come help him. As Bohemond's messenger came into our camps, everyone grabbed their horses and weapons and strove to reach the enemy. As soon as Suleiman and his men knew that our army had joined in the battle against him, he despaired of victory and surrendered to flight. Thus he who had taken many captives and tents from Bohemond's camps had by God's strength abandoned them all.

Some reported an amazing miracle, although we didn't see it.[2] Two horsemen with shining arms and wondrous countenances rode at the head of our army, thus menacing the enemy and leaving them with no capacity for fighting. To those Turks who did try to pierce them with

[1] That is, from Raymond of Saint-Gilles, Adhémar of Le Puy, and Godfrey of Bouillon.

[2] "We" in this case refers to Raymond and his collaborator Pons of Balazun, a knight who worked with him on the first sections of his chronicle but who died before the crusade reached Jerusalem.

Raymond of Aguilers, *Liber*, ed. John H. Hill and Laurita L. Hill Introduction and notes trans. Philippe Wolff (Paris: P. Geuthner, 1969), 45–46. Translated by the author.

lances, they seemed invulnerable.[3] These stories we learned from former enemies who subsequently joined us. And we can add one detail as evidence: Over the next two days we found enemy horses and their riders lying dead on the road.

[3]This is the earliest apparent reference to saints fighting alongside the crusaders. The ones most frequently named as joining the army were George, Theodore, and Demetrius.

31

BISHOP ADHÉMAR OF LE PUY AND PATRIARCH SIMEON OF JERUSALEM

The Road to Antioch

October 1097

In addition to discussing recent events and practical difficulties—describing, for example, how the Franks began forming alliances with local Christian (primarily Armenian) communities—this letter suggests, in the excerpt included here, that the crusaders and their spiritual counselors were developing new interpretations of Urban II's original indulgence and its connection to the idea of martyrdom.

Simeon, Patriarch of Jerusalem, and Adhémar, Bishop of St. Mary of Le Puy (the one to whom Pope Urban especially entrusted the welfare of the Christian army), blessings, peace, and eternal salvation to you from our God and Lord Jesus Christ!

By common counsel we write to you—clerics, monks, and bishops as well as dukes, counts, and all other good laymen. Earnestly praying for the salvation of your souls, all of us now command all of you who inhabit northern climes not to delay coming to us. Let all those come who wish to do so for their own salvation and who have sufficient bodily health

---

Heinrich Hagenmeyer, *Die Kreuzzugsbriefe aus den Jahren 1088–1100* (Hildesheim: Georg Olms, 1901), ep. 6, 141–42. Translated by the author.

as well as the means to undertake the journey. You can come to us with only a few possessions, for Almighty God will look to your livelihood.

Dearest brothers, we Christians are in Romania. We have conquered the great city of Nicaea, albeit with great difficulty. From Nicaea our army is moving toward Antioch, and we have conquered many other cities and Turkish castles. We have 100,000 cavalry and foot soldiers, but to what end? We are few when compared to the pagans. But God truly fights for us. And on this point, brothers, listen to this miracle that the most holy patriarch sends to all Christians. The Lord appeared to him in a vision and promised to those toiling on this journey that each of them would wear a crown as they processed before him on the dreadful final day of judgment.[1]

You know well that anyone who took the sign of the holy cross and stayed behind is excommunicated because of his apostasy. By the power of the same holy cross and the sepulcher of the Lord, we adjure and beseech you[2] to strike all of them with the sword of anathema unless they hasten to follow us so that while we are in Romania they will be here by next year.

Farewell! Remember and pray for us, who struggle day and night.

[1] The crown symbolizes martyrdom, which means that everyone in the army will be counted as a martyr and receive salvation on Judgment Day.

[2] Presumably, European bishops and especially the pope.

5

Antioch: Where the Crusade Became a Holy War

32

COUNT STEPHEN OF BLOIS

The Siege of Antioch: A Letter from Count Stephen of Blois

March 1098

Stephen of Blois's earlier prediction that the armies would reach Jerusalem in five weeks, if not delayed at Antioch (see Document 28), proved accurate. The crusading host did not, in fact, reach Antioch until nearly four months later, on October 20, 1097, and the outcome of the siege would not be resolved for another eight months. Despite the incredibly harsh conditions the crusaders faced, Stephen remained confident, as this letter, written in March 1098, demonstrates.

Count Stephen sends the blessing and grace of salvation to Adele, his sweetest, most beloved wife, to his dearest children, and to all his followers great and small.

You may surely believe, dearest, that this messenger whom I have sent to your sweetness left me safe and healthy and enriched by good fortune at Antioch, which now the chosen army of Christ has been besieging in the name of Lord Jesus for twenty-three straight weeks. Rest assured, my love, that I have now doubled the gold, silver, and other riches that

Heinrich Hagenmeyer, *Die Kreuzzugsbriefe aus den Jahren 1088–1100* (Hildesheim: Georg Olms, 1901), ep. 10, 149–52. Translated by the author.

your sweetness handed over to me when I left you. For after taking counsel, all our princes have now established me (reluctant though I am!) as lord of the whole army and overseer and governor of their every deed.

You have heard already that after the capture of Nicaea we fought no small battle against the treacherous Turks and that with God's help we laid them low.[1] Afterward we gained for the Lord all parts of Romania and then Cappadocia. In Cappadocia, we learned that there lived a Turkish prince named Assam, so we directed our path toward him. We manfully conquered all of his castles and chased him into a well-fortified castle atop a high ridge. We gave Assam's land to one of our princes, and to help him subdue the aforesaid Assam, we left him there with many Christian knights. From there we continued to chase the wicked Turks through Armenia, eventually driving them to the great river Euphrates and forcing them to the riverbank. Abandoning their packs and packhorses, they fled across the river into Arabia. The bolder of the Turkish knights set a swift course night and day into Syria and hastened to enter the royal city of Antioch ahead of us. The whole army of God knew how they fled and gave due thanks and praise to the Lord.

We thus hastened joyfully to the aforesaid capital city of Antioch and besieged it. There we have had many conflicts with the Turks. In truth we have fought seven battles against the citizens of Antioch and against countless fierce souls who came to bring help to them, with Christ marching before us. With the Lord our God's assistance, we were victorious all seven times, and truly we killed more of them than one could count! In these battles and in many other encounters around the city, to be sure, they killed many of our Christian coreligionists, whose souls they helped raise to paradise.

Antioch is a city great beyond belief, one we have found most powerful and invincible. More than five thousand bold Turkish knights have gathered in the city, not counting Saracens, Paulicians, Arabs, Turcopoles, Syrians, Armenians, and various other nations, comprising an infinite multitude. Thus far we have endured much toil and countless evils because of our adversaries and God's enemies. Many have now used up all their goods in this sacred struggle. Indeed, many of our Franks would have suffered physical death from hunger if God's clemency and our money had not come to the rescue! Throughout the whole winter in front of this city we have endured brutal cold and unbearably heavy rainfall in the name of Christ our Lord. It is false what some say about the unbearable heat of the Syrian sun, for their winter is similar to ours in the West.

[1] A reference to the Battle of Dorylaeum, described in Documents 29 and 30.

When Caspian, the emir of Antioch (emir means "prince" and "lord"), saw how much he was suffering because of us, he sent his son, named Sensadolus, to the prince who holds Jerusalem and to the prince Calap Rodoan and to the prince of Damascus. He also sent him into Arabia to see Bolianuth and to Khorasan to see Hamelnuth.[2] These five emirs with twelve thousand chosen Turkish soldiers suddenly came to attempt to relieve Antioch. In ignorance of all this, we had scattered many of our knights around the cities and castles. Indeed, in Syria now there are 165 cities and castles under our control. A little before they reached the city, however, we went out to meet them, going about three leagues with seven hundred knights onto a plain near the Iron Bridge.[3] God fought for us, his faithful men, against them, and on that day through God's virtue we laid low our enemies in battle, and because God always fights for us, we killed more of them than you could count. To celebrate the victory, Christ's people gathered two hundred of their heads and carried them back to the army. Also, the emperor of Babylon sent his Saracen messengers to our army with a letter and through it he secured peace and amity with us.[4]

Now, dearest one, I'd like to tell you want happened to us during Lent. Our princes decided that a tower should be built before one of the city gates that lies between our camps and the sea. The Turks had been coming out of that gate every day and killing our men who went to the sea. (The city of Antioch lies five leagues from the sea.) For this reason they sent that outstanding man Bohemond, Count Raymond of Saint-Gilles, and sixty knights to the sea to lead back sailors who might help with this project. But when they were bringing the sailors back to us, an army of Turks that had gathered together caught our two princes unawares and drove them into a harried flight. In this panicked flight that I am describing, we lost more than five hundred of our foot soldiers to the glory of God. From our knights we only lost two that I know of.[5]

On that same day we went out to receive our brothers joyfully, completely ignorant of their misfortune. As we neared the aforesaid city gate, a crowd of Antiochene knights and foot soldiers, glorying in their

[2] Yaghi-Siyan was the emir of Damascus. His son was named Shams ad-Dawla. The lords referred to here are Ilghazi in Jerusalem, Ridwan of Aleppo, and Duqaq of Damascus. Bolianuth and Hamelnuth are less certain.

[3] This battle occurred on February 9, 1098. Contrary to what Stephen says here, the army was led only by Ridwan of Aleppo. Six weeks earlier, Frankish soldiers had unexpectedly met up with a relief force led by Duqaq of Damascus.

[4] Babylon here refers to Egypt, governed by the Fatimids, who, as Shia Muslims, were the confessional and political enemies of the Turks. After the siege of Nicaea, Alexius had arranged for the Franks to send ambassadors to Cairo.

[5] This battle occurred on March 29, 1098.

triumph, fell upon us. Seeing them, we sent word to the Christian camps that everyone needed to join us and to be prepared for battle. Our men thus came together, even as the disoriented princes Bohemond and Raymond came back with what remained of their followers and told of the awful thing that had happened to them. This terrible news filled us with fury against the blasphemous Turks. Ready to die for Christ and saddened for our brothers, we assembled hastily. God's enemies and ours fled from us, trying to get back into their city, but by God's grace things went differently from what they had planned. For as they tried to cross the bridge built over the great river Moscholo,[6] we pursued them closely and killed many of them before they reached the bridge. Many others we cast into the river, all of whom died. Others still we killed while crossing the bridge or else in front of the gate.

I tell you, my dear, and you can be sure it's true, that in this single battle we killed thirty emirs (that is, "princes") and three hundred other noble Turkish knights, not counting other Turks and pagans. Added all up, the number of Turkish and Saracen dead is 1,230. We did not even lose one of our men.

While my chaplain, Alexander, was hastily writing this letter, some of our men laid a trap for the Turks and defeated them in combat, through God's help. They killed sixty of them and brought their heads back to the army.

These are but a few of the details I am writing to you, my dearest, and since I cannot express to you what is in my heart, dearest, I ask of you that you do well, take good care of your land, and treat your sons and your men fairly, as is proper, since you will surely see me as soon as I am able.

Farewell!

[6] In fact, the Orontes.

33

The Fall of Antioch

ca. 1100

Toward the end of May 1098, the crusaders learned that a massive Turkish relief force was fast approaching Antioch. It seemed that the crusaders would either have to flee Antioch (which Stephen of Blois did) or else hold their camps and face near-certain destruction. But as the armies would soon learn, Bohemond of Taranto was as skilled at diplomacy and treachery as he was at battlefield leadership. Bohemond's decisions and conduct would seem to be not above reproach, though the anonymous writer (who was apparently a member of Bohemond's retinue) appears to try to put these events in the best possible light.

There was an emir of the Turks named Pirrus who struck up a very close friendship with Bohemond. Bohemond frequently approached him through messengers in the hopes of being received warmly in the city. He offered Pirrus the Christian faith and promised to make him rich and much honored.

Pirrus agreed to these words and promises, saying, "I oversee three towers, which I promise freely to Bohemond, and I will receive him in them at whatever time he might choose."

Bohemond felt reassured about getting into the city. Happy, with a tranquil mind and a pleasant demeanor, he went to the other leaders and spoke jokingly to them, saying, "Gentlemen, wise warriors, just look at how poor and miserable we all are, no matter whether one is important or not! And we don't know when or how things will improve for us. Therefore, if it seems good and fair to you, one of us should offer himself to the others, and if in any way or by any stratagem he could acquire or purloin the city, by himself or with the help of others, let us agree unanimously to give him the city as a gift."

Everyone forbade the idea and rejected it, saying, "This city should be given to no one person, but we all ought to hold it equally. We have all shared in the labor, and thus we ought to have an equal reward."

The Deeds of the Franks and the Other Pilgrims to Jerusalem, ed. Rosalind Hill (London: T. Nelson, 1962), 44–48. Translated by the author.

Hearing these words, Bohemond smiled a little less and withdrew.

Not long afterward we heard reports about an enemy army—Turks, Paulicians, Agulani, Azymites, and many other nations.[1] Our leaders immediately met together and held another council, saying that if Bohemond could obtain the city either by himself or with the help of others, then we should freely and unanimously give it to him, with one proviso: if the emperor would fulfill every pact he had promised and pledged to us and come to help us, then we would rightfully give it to him. Otherwise, Bohemond could hold it under his own authority.

Immediately Bohemond humbly and regularly entreated his friend, abjectly promising him great and delightful rewards thusly: "Behold! The perfect time is before us to bring about whatever good thing we might wish. Therefore, help me now, my friend Pirrus!" Rather pleased at this news, Pirrus said that he was going to assist him as he ought. The following night he sent his son to Bohemond as a pledge, so that Bohemond might feel more secure about entering the city.[2] He also sent a message to the effect that that evening Bohemond should summon all the Franks and pretend that they were heading into the land of the Saracens for the sake of plunder before returning swiftly through the mountains on the right-hand side of the city. "And I will keep a close watch for those troops to welcome them into the towers I hold under my power and guardianship."

Bohemond ordered one of his servants, called "Bad-Head," to come to him quickly, and he directed him to act as his herald and call together a great number of Franks so that they might ingenuously prepare to journey to Saracen lands. And so it happened. Bohemond entrusted his plan to Duke Godfrey, the Count of Flanders, the Count of Saint-Gilles, and the bishop of Le Puy, saying, "With God's help, Antioch will be surrendered to us tonight!"

All things were then set in order. Knights held the plain and foot soldiers the mountain, riding and walking almost to dawn, and then they drew near to the towers where the watchman was keeping guard. Bohemond dismounted and gave orders to everyone, saying, "Go forth with a confident mind and happy in your company! Climb up the ladder into Antioch, which we will possess immediately, God willing." They went to the ladder, which was now raised up and fastened to the city walls, and

[1] The names are fanciful. Paulicians and Azymites were in fact Christian sects.

[2] Other versions of this story say that Bohemond had captured Pirrus's son and was holding him hostage in exchange for the soldier's cooperation.

about sixty of our men climbed up it and dispersed through the towers under Pirrus's guard.

When Pirrus saw that so few of our men had climbed the ladder, he grew worried, afraid for himself and for our men, lest they fall into the Turks' hands. And he said, "Micró Francos echomé!"[3] That means, "We have few Franks!" "Where is fierce Bohemond? Where is that invincible man?"

Meanwhile, a Lombard servant climbed down the ladder, hurried as fast as he could to Bohemond, and said, "Why are you just standing there, smart man? Why did you come here? Look! We already have three towers!"

Thus inspired, Bohemond and some other men went joyfully to the ladder. When our men on the towers saw them, they began calling out in lighthearted tones, "God wills it!" We were shouting the same thing.

Now they climbed the ladder in a marvelous fashion. They climbed and they rushed into other towers. They dealt death to anyone they found. They even killed Pirrus's brother.

In the meantime, by an unfortunate chance, the ladder our men had been climbing broke, causing terrible grief and sadness to well up in us. Although the ladder had been broken, nevertheless there was a locked door to the left of us which few of us could see, for it was nighttime. But we looked for it by feeling around and found it, and everyone rushed to it. We broke the gate and entered through it.

Then an outcry resounded through the city. Bohemond paid it no mind. Instead he ordered his estimable banner to be carried to the mountain near the citadel.[4] Everyone in the city was screaming at once. Day was breaking. Those of our men who were in tents outside the city heard the violent outcry. They hastily left their tents and saw Bohemond's banner atop the mountain, and everyone rushed forward and passed through the city gates. And they killed the Turks and Saracens they found there, except for those who fled into the citadel. Other Turks exited through the gates and ran and thus escaped alive.

Their lord Yaghi-Siyan, in terrible fear of the Franks, gave himself heedlessly to flight, along with many others who were with him. His path took him into Tancred's territory not far from the city. Their horses

[3]The chronicler adds a note of credibility to the scene by quoting Pirrus in Greek, suggesting the language that he and Bohemond may have been negotiating in.

[4]The city of Antioch is built onto the slopes of mountains, and the medieval walls incorporated these mountains into the defenses. One of the walls included a massive citadel, which the crusaders failed to take during this attack.

were exhausted, so they headed to a village and hid inside a house. The Syrian and Armenian people who lived on that mountain recognized him and quickly captured him. They cut his head off and offered it to Bohemond as a present in hopes that they might earn their liberty as a result. His belt and scabbard were worth sixty bezants.

All of this happened on the third day in the month of June, a Thursday. All the city squares everywhere were full of dead corpses, so that no one was able to endure the great stench. No one could walk through a city street without stepping on dead corpses.

34

IBN AL-ATHIR

An Arab Historian's Account of the Fall of Antioch

Early Thirteenth Century

By the time of the fall of Antioch, Arab observers were taking notice of the Franks, though it is unclear if they fully grasped the religious character of crusading warfare. The following account, based on earlier written evidence, is from a grand Arabic history of the Islamic world by Ibn al-Athir (1160–1233). While Ibn al-Athir lived well after the events he describes, he had access to a wide array of written and oral sources. The care with which he assembled his evidence is impressive. In a very short space, he describes the entire eight-month siege of Antioch. While he confirms the general outline of the story told in Document 33, he does so with a sympathetic eye toward the attempts of the emir Yaghi-Siyan to save his city.

When the ruler Yaghi-Siyan heard of their coming, he feared the Christians in the city.[1] He sent out the Muslim inhabitants by themselves and ordered them to dig the moat. Then the next day he sent out the

[1] As a former Byzantine capital on the frontier, Antioch had a substantial Christian population, most of them following creeds unfamiliar to the crusaders.

The Chronicle of Ibn al-Athir for the Crusading Period from al-Kamil fi'l-ta'rikh, trans. D. S. Richards (Surrey, U.K.: Ashgate, 2005), 1:14–15.

Christians also to dig the moat, unaccompanied by any Muslim. They laboured on it until the evening but when they wished to enter the city he prevented them and said, "You can give me Antioch until I see how things will be with us and the Franks." They asked, "Who will look after our sons and our wives?" "I will look after them in your place," he replied. So they held back and took up residence in the Frankish camp. The Franks besieged the city for nine months. Yaghi-Siyan displayed such courage, excellent counsel, resolution and careful planning as had never been seen from anyone else. Most of the Franks perished. Had they remained in the numbers they set out with, they would have overwhelmed the lands of Islam. Yaghi-Siyan protected the families of those Christians of Antioch, whom he had expelled, and restrained the hands that would do them harm.

After their siege of Antioch had lasted long, the Franks made contact with one of the men garrisoning the towers, who was an armourer, known as Ruzbah, and offered him money and grants of land. He was in charge of a tower next to the valley, which was built with a window overlooking the valley. After they had made an arrangement with this cursed armourer, they came to the window, which they opened and through which they entered. A large number climbed up on ropes. When they numbered more than five hundred, they blew the trumpet. That was at dawn. The defenders were already tired from many sleepless nights on guard. Yaghi-Siyan awoke and asked what was happening. He was told, "That trumpet is from the citadel. No doubt it has already been taken." However, it was not from the citadel but merely from that tower. He was seized with fear, opened the city gate and left in headlong flight with thirty retainers. His deputy as governor of the city came and asked after him. He was told that he had fled, so he himself fled by another gate. That was a boon for the Franks. Had he held firm for a while, they would have perished. The Franks entered the city through the gate and sacked it, killing the Muslims that were there. This was in Juamda I [April–May 1098].[2]

When the next day dawned, Yaghi-Siyan came to his senses again. He had been like one distraught. He looked at himself after he had covered several leagues and said to those with him, "Where am I?" "Four leagues from Antioch," he was told. He then regretted his flight to safety and his failure to fight until he either drove them from the city or was himself killed. He started to lament and bewail having abandoned his wife, his children and the Muslim population. Because of the violence of what

[2] The city fell on the night of June 2/3.

afflicted him he fell from his horse in a faint. When he fell to the ground, his followers went to remount him but he could not hold on, for he was close to death. They therefore left him and rode away. An Armenian who was cutting firewood and came across him when he was at his last gasp, killed him, cut off his head and took it to the Franks at Antioch.

35

The New Enemy: Kerbogah

ca. 1100

The Latin Christians would have known very little about Kerbogah's personality, and yet they found him immensely fascinating. Participants in the crusade liked to imagine him storming arrogantly around his camp, boasting how he would destroy or enslave all the Franks. Latin historians also liked to imagine an occasional voice of sanity trying to dissuade him. This voice usually belonged to Kerbogah's mother, who in Latin histories visits her son's camp and warns him that God and prophecy together will deny him success in battle.

Kerbogah's mother was in the city of Aleppo, and she came at once to him and said tearfully, "Son, surely what I'm hearing isn't true!"

He said to her, "What?"

She said, "I have heard that you want to make war with the nation of the Franks."

He said, "Your information is correct."

She said, "I swear to you, son, by the names of all the gods and by your own goodness, don't make war with the Franks. You are an unconquered knight, never known to flee in defeat from the field of battle. Your army's fame is known everywhere, and every prudent knight trembles at the mention of your name. Son, I know well you are a great and powerful warrior and no Christian or pagan nation can stand before your gaze. At the mention of your name they can only flee, as if from a

The Deeds of the Franks and the Other Pilgrims to Jerusalem, ed. Rosalind Hill (London: T. Nelson, 1962), 53–56. Translated by the author.

raging lion! And so I ask you, dearest son, that you accept my advice and not entertain further thoughts or ideas of going to war against the Christians."

Kerbogah heard his mother's warning and answered savagely: "What are you talking about, mother? I think that you're crazy, or possessed by the Furies! Look! I have with me as many emirs as there are Christians great and small!"

His mother answered him, "O, sweetest son! The Christians cannot contend with you. I know that they cannot bring the fight to you. But their God fights for them daily, and every day and night he shelters and defends them and watches over them as a shepherd watches over his flocks. He does not allow any other people to harm or trouble them, and whoever wishes to resist them their same God opposes them, as he said through the voice of the prophet David: 'Scatter the nations that wish for war!' Or elsewhere: 'Pour your wrath over the nations who do not know you and who in their kingdoms do not call upon your name!'[1] Before they make preparations for battle, their omnipotent warrior God and his saints have already conquered their enemies. How much more will he do to you who, as his enemy, has prepared to resist him with all your strength? You know this is a true statement, my dearest, that these Christians are called 'sons of Christ,' and that the voice of the prophet called them 'sons of adoption and promise.' According to the Apostle they are Christ's heirs, to whom Christ has given a promised inheritance, in the words of the prophet: 'Your boundaries shall be from the rising to the setting sun, and no one will stand against you.'[2] Is anyone able to gainsay or challenge these verses? But if you engage them in battle, you will suffer tremendous loss and shame, you will lose many of your faithful knights, and you will be deprived of all the spoils that you have captured. In terror you will flee. You will not die in this battle, however, but you will die within the year. This God when angered against an outlaw does not impose immediate judgment, but he punishes him with public retribution whenever he wishes. And so I fear that he will sentence you with a severe judgment. You will not die, I say, but you will nevertheless lose everything you have."

Kerbogah grieved deeply in his heart at his mother's words and said to her, "Dearest mother, I ask you who told you these things about the Christian nation, that their God loves them so, and that he possesses

[1] Psalms 68:31 and 79:6.

[2] "The Apostle" is St. Paul. The quotation does not precisely match any biblical passage.

such great power in battle, and that the Christians will conquer us in the battle of Antioch, and that they will capture our spoils and that they will pursue us in great victory, and that this very year I will die a sudden death?"

His grief-stricken mother answered, "Dearest son, behold! More than one hundred years ago it was found in our scripture and in the books of the gentiles that the Christian nation would come against us and would always conquer us, that they would rule over the pagans, and that our people would be made subject to them.[3] I don't know whether these things will happen now or in the future. In sadness I have come to you from the beautiful city of Aleppo, where through observations and sophisticated incantations I have studied the stars in heaven and sagely examined the planets, along with the twelve signs of the Zodiac and many other oracles. In all of them I found that the Christians will conquer us everywhere, and I fear that I'll know unbearable sadness because of you, should I survive you."

Kerbogah said to her, "Dearest mother, tell me about all the unbelievable things now in my heart."

She said, "I will gladly do so, dearest son, if I know anything unfamiliar to you."

He said to her, "Are not Bohemond and Tancred gods of the Franks, and do they not free them from their enemies? And do they eat 2,000 cows and 4,000 pigs in one sitting?"

His mother answered, "Dearest son, Bohemond and Tancred are mortal men like all others, but their God loves them especially before all others and has given them power in battle above all others. For their God's name is 'Almighty.' He made the heavens and the earth and created the seas and all things therein. His throne has been eternally ready in heaven, his power everywhere feared."

Her son said, "If that is the case, I will not put off fighting them."

[3] "Our scripture" is presumably a reference to the Qur'an. "The books of the gentiles" could refer to prophecies in the tradition of Pseudo-Methodius, one version of which is attributed to the Roman Tirburtine Sibyl.

36

FULCHER OF CHARTRES

Two Visions Preceding the Battle with Kerbogah

ca. 1106

As conditions inside Antioch grew more desperate, some members of the crusading army began to report experiencing miraculous visions. Fulcher of Chartres, a priest who had begun the crusade but had then abandoned the main army and settled in the city of Edessa, describes two of these visions, one seen by a priest, named elsewhere as Stephen of Valence, and the other by an unnamed crusader. Both men were planning to abandon the siege, but the visions restored their courage.

But at that time the Lord did not forget his people. Rather, he appeared often to many of them, as they themselves confirmed. For reassurance, he promised that they would soon rejoice in victory.

The Lord appeared to a cleric who was running away in fear of death and said to him, "Where are you going, brother?"

"I'm running away lest I die," he answered. "Thus many flee to avoid a wicked death."

The Lord answered, "Don't run away! Go back! For on the day of battle I will be there with those who persevere. The prayers of my mother have appeased my anger toward them. Because of their sins, they will come close to dying. Let their hope remain fixed on me, though, and I will give them triumph over the Turks. Repent and be saved! It is the Lord who speaks to you!"

This man quickly returned and told what he had heard.

Meanwhile, at that time many were hoping to climb down the wall using ropes and escape, and several actually did so because they feared death from hunger or the sword.[1] As one of them descended, his dead brother appeared to him and said, "Where are you fleeing to, brother?

[1] A twelfth-century writer named Orderic Vitalis says that these people, upon returning home, were ridiculed as "Secret Ropedancers."

Fulcher of Chartres, *Historia Hierosolymitana*, ed. Heinrich Hagenmeyer (Heidelberg: Carl Winter, 1913), 244–47. Translated by the author.

Stay! Fear not! The Lord will be with you, as will your companions who have preceded you in death. They will fight alongside you against the Turks."

The man marveled at the dead man's words. Abandoning his escape attempt, he told others what had happened.

Although it pleased the Lord to relieve his servants, who could not bear any more misery and who did not have anything to eat, leaving them and their horses terribly weakened, the people nonetheless ordered a universal three-day fast with prayers and acts of charity, so that by these penances and supplications, they might mollify their God.

37

RAYMOND OF AGUILERS

The Discovery of the Holy Lance of Antioch

ca. 1100

Raymond of Aguilers, the chaplain of Count Raymond of Saint-Gilles, was intimately involved in the discovery of the Holy Lance, the relic with which the Roman soldier Longinus pierced Christ's side on the cross. Most of this selection is written in the voice of Peter Bartholomew, the nearly illiterate priest whose visions led to the discovery of the Holy Lance in Antioch. The chronicler Raymond, as Peter Bartholomew's protector and chief advocate, seems to have taken care to record the visionary's story and to put it in the best possible light.

The Discovery of the Lance Begins

After the capture of the city of Antioch, the Lord through his power and benevolence chose a poor rustic, born in Provence, to reassure all and to give a message to the count and the bishop of Le Puy:[1]

[1] Raymond of Saint-Gilles and Bishop Adhémar. Peter speaks directly to these two men frequently during his presentation.

Raymond of Aguilers, *Liber*, ed. John H. Hill and Laurita L. Hill (Paris: P. Geuthner, 1969), 68–71, 75. Translated by the author.

Andrew, the apostle of God and our Lord Jesus Christ, commanded and ordered me four times to come to you once you had conquered the city and to deliver to you the lance that pierced our Savior's side. Today, when I was with the others fighting outside the city walls, I was caught between two horses and nearly suffocated and tried to retreat.[2] I sat down on a stone there, as if lifeless. Saddened and reeling from grief and fear, Blessed Andrew with a companion came to me and threatened me gravely if I did not swiftly render unto you the lance.

When the count and the bishop requested that he set out in order what had been revealed and commanded to him, he said:

During the first earthquake which happened at Antioch,[3] while the Franks were besieging it, I was seized by such a great fear that the only words I could form were, "God help me!" It was night and I was lying down, and there was no one in my little hut whose company might reassure me. As I said, the earthquake lasted a long time and my fear kept growing, when suddenly two men stood before me clad in shining robes. One of them was older and of medium height, and he had graying red hair, black eyes that suited his face, and a long, bushy white beard. The other was younger and taller and fairer in appearance than the children of men.

The older one said to me, "What are you doing?"

I was especially fearful, since I did not know who had come to me, so I answered, "Who are you?"

He said, "Get up. Don't be afraid. And listen to what I have to tell you. I am the apostle Andrew. Bring together the bishop of Le Puy, the Count of Saint-Gilles, and Peter Raymond of Hautpol, and say this to them: 'Why does the bishop fail to preach and to warn the people and bless the people every day with the cross that he carries? It would surely be a great boon to them.'"

And he continued, "Come with me and I will show you the lance of our Father Jesus Christ, which you will give to the count. For God set it aside for him at the time that he was born."

I rose and followed him into the city wearing nothing but my nightshirt, and he guided me through the northern door into the Church of Blessed Peter the Apostle, which the Saracens had turned into a Mahomerie.[4] In this church there were two lamps giving out so much light that it seemed to be midday. And he said to me, "Look here." And

[2] The pitched battle occurred on June 10, 1098.
[3] December 30, 1097.
[4] A mosque.

he ordered me to stand next to the column nearest the steps leading to the south side of the altar, with his companion at some distance from the altar.

St. Andrew slipped under the earth and produced a lance and held it out to me in his hands. And he said to me, "Behold! The lance that pierced his side, whence the salvation of the whole world flowed!"[5]

As I held it in my hands and wept tears of joy, I said to him, "Lord, if you want, I will carry it and hand it over to the count."

He said to me, "Not now. The capture of the city is still in the future. At that time you will come here with twelve men, and you will look for it in the place where I withdrew it and where I now return it." And he returned it.

After taking care of this business, he led me back over the city wall and into my house, and then they withdrew from me. I started thinking, comparing my impoverished dress to your great finery, and I feared to approach you.

Some time afterward, I had gone looking for sustenance to a fortress near Edessa. On the first day of Lent, just as the cock crowed, Blessed Andrew appeared in the same robes and with the same companion who had previously come to me, and a great light filled the house.[6] And Blessed Andrew said, "Are you awake?"

Awakened by him, I answered, "No, Lord. My Lord, I'm not sleeping."

And he said to me, "Have you said what I earlier ordered you to say?"

And I answered, "Lord, haven't I prayed for you to send someone else? Out of fear because of my poverty, I hesitate to approach them."[7]

And he said to me, "Don't you know why God has called upon all of you, and how much he loves you, and how he selected you especially? He has made you come here to avenge the sufferings of his people and the scorn heaped upon him. He loves you so much that the saints now at rest want to come back in the flesh to fight with us, because they have learned what divine dispensation has set aside for you. God has chosen you from all peoples just as grains of wheat are gathered from the oats, and by his grace and merits you have surpassed all who came before you or shall come later, just as the price of gold surpasses that of silver."

They withdrew, and afterward I fell into such an illness that I lost my sight and started to make arrangements to dispose of my meager possessions. Then I realized that I deserved these sufferings because I

[5] Blood and water flowed from Christ's side, emblematic of the Eucharist and baptism.

[6] The vision occurred on February 10, 1098. About ten days after the vision, Godfrey of Bouillon's brother arrived in Edessa as a mercenary and shortly thereafter made himself count of the city.

[7] Count Raymond and Bishop Adhémar.

had neglected the apostle's commands. Thus comforted, I returned to the siege.

Again, thinking about the handicap of my poverty, I started to fear that if I were to approach you, you would think that I was starving and you would declare that I said such things only to get food. I therefore kept silent.

Some time later, on the eve of Palm Sunday, I was at the port St. Simeon with my lord William Peter, resting in a tent. Blessed Andrew appeared, with the same robe and the same companion, and he spoke to me: "Why haven't you said what I directed you to say to the count and the bishop and the others?"

And I answered, "Lord, didn't I pray to you to send someone else instead of me—someone who is wiser and whom they would be willing to listen to? Besides, there are Turks coming and going and killing on the road!"

St. Andrew said, "Fear not! Nothing will harm you. Also say these things to the count: When he comes to the river Jordan, he should avoid getting wet and should cross it in a boat. When he has crossed it, while clad in a shirt and linen breeches, he shall be sprinkled with water from the river. Once the clothes have dried, he shall set them aside with the lance of the Lord."

[After yet another delay and the skirmish outside the walls described earlier, Peter Bartholomew's story continues, now told in the voice of the chronicler Raymond of Aguilers.]

On the appointed day, the necessary preparations completed, twelve men with the one who had spoken about the lance began to dig, once everyone else had been expelled from the church. Among those twelve men were the bishop of Orange; Count Raymond's chaplain (who wrote these words); the count Pons of Balazun;[8] and Ferald of Thouars. At sunset, after digging from dawn till dusk, some of us began to lose faith that we would ever find the lance. The count in fact had already left to guard a castle. But we had recruited other people as replacements for him and for those who had given in to fatigue to continue digging, and they manfully kept working. The young man who had spoken about the lance[9] saw that we were exhausted, so he took off his shoes and trousers and clad only in his shirt jumped into the pit and exhorted us to

[8] The knight Pons is identified at the beginning of the chronicle as Raymond's collaborator.

[9] Peter Bartholomew.

beseech God to reveal his lance as a sign of reassurance and victory to his people. Finally, moved by his own pious grace, the Lord showed us his lance. And when I who am writing these things saw only the tip of it, I kissed it.

So much joy and exultation filled the city that I cannot describe it. The lance was found on June 14. On the next night Blessed Andrew appeared to the young man through whom the lance had been revealed and said to him, "Behold! God gave the count what he always intended for him and no one else, and God has made him the standard-bearer for the army."

38

A Final Parley with Kerbogah

ca. 1100

Reassured by the discovery of the Holy Lance, or else willing to exploit the army's belief in it, the leaders of the crusade decided on a daring plan: They would leave the city en masse and take the fight to Kerbogah. Before the battle, however, they made one final effort to strike a truce with him, entrusting this delicate mission to Peter the Hermit. Our source again is the anonymous author whose leader, Bohemond, is usually credited with playing the key part in this stage of the crusade.

Then our leaders decided in a meeting that they would send to Christ's enemies the Turks a messenger who would through an interpreter ask them with an assured eloquence why they had so arrogantly entered into the land of the Christians, why they had set camps there, and why they were killing and conquering Christ's servants. When they brought their meeting to an end, they found two men, Peter the Hermit and Herluin, and they said all this to them: "Go to this contemptible contingent of Turks and carefully explain all these things to them, and ask them why they have boldly and arrogantly entered the Christians' land, our land."

The Deeds of the Franks and the Other Pilgrims to Jerusalem, ed. Rosalind Hill (London: T. Nelson, 1962), 65–67. Translated by the author.

Under these instructions, the messengers withdrew and went to that ungodly gathering and thusly related all these messages to Kerbogah and others: "Our leaders and elders are greatly astonished that you would boldly and arrogantly enter into Christian land and their land. We think and believe—possibly—that you have come here because you want to become Christians. Or maybe you have come here because you want to wrong the Christians in every way possible. All the same, our leaders ask you at once to leave God's land and the Christians' land, where Blessed Peter once converted to the worship of Christ through his preaching. And they will allow you to take all of your possessions with you—horses and mules, asses and camels, and sheep and cows, and all your other valuables they will allow you to take with you wherever you wish."

Then Kerbogah, the prince of the prideful sultan of Persia's army, with all his other men, answered threateningly: "We neither desire your God nor want your Christianity, and we spit on them and you! We have come here out of astonishment that your elders and leaders whom you mention call this land, which we conquered from effeminate races, 'their land.' You wish to know what we say to you? Go back right away and tell your elders that if they desire to become Turks in all things and if they wish to renounce your God whom you submissively worship and to repudiate your laws, then we will give to them this land and more than enough from our land, including cities and castles such that none of you will stay foot soldiers, but all of you will become knights and be like us, and we will always hold them to be the closest of friends. Otherwise, let them know that they will all be punished by death, or else led in chains to Khorasan where they will be forever throughout all time the captive slaves of us and our children."

Our envoys returned to the city swiftly, reporting everything that this cruel people had said to them. It is said that Herluin knew their language and was the interpreter for Peter the Hermit.

39

RAYMOND OF AGUILERS

The Battle with Kerbogah

ca. 1100

All medieval chroniclers believed the victory over Kerbogah was something of a miracle. Modern military historians have attempted to come up with a more rational explanation for the Franks' success, but the task is difficult. How did a force as spent and starved as the crusaders manage to overcome a superior, well-fed, and well-rested adversary? The chaplain Raymond of Aguilers was not just an eyewitness to these events. He in fact accompanied Bishop Adhémar onto the field of battle.

When the day of battle came, someone was needed to guard the city against the people in the citadel while everyone else set out to fight. They built a stone wall and a rampart on the slope of our mountain to defend against the enemy, and they fortified it with petraries[1] and entrusted it to two hundred men led by Count Raymond, who was sick unto death.

The day of the fight had arrived. In the morning everyone received the Eucharist and offered themselves to die for the honor of the Roman church, the nation of the Franks, and God, if he should wish. They went out to war in this way: There were two double lines composed of followers of the count and the bishop.[2] The foot soldiers, whom the knights preceded, would go or stay according to the princes' commands, while the knights would follow them and guard them from behind. A similar arrangement was made for Bohemond and Tancred's people; also for the people of the Count of Normandy and the French count; also with

[1] A type of catapult.
[2] Raymond of Saint-Gilles and Adhémar of Le Puy. Raymond of Aguilers, the author, was in this division.

Raymond of Aguilers, *Liber*, ed. John H. Hill and Laurita L. Hill (Paris: P. Geuthner, 1969), 79–83. Translated by the author.

the people of the duke and the Burgundians.[3] Heralds went through the city proclaiming that each man needed to adhere to his particular prince. It was decided that Hugh the Great, the Count of Flanders, and the Count of Normandy would march first to battle, then the duke, after the duke the bishop, and after the bishop, Bohemond. Everyone gathered together, each man before his banner and with his kin group, within the city and in front of the bridge gate.

O, how blessed the nation whose Lord is its God! O, how blessed the people whom God has chosen! O, how changed is the demeanor of this army, from sadness into enthusiasm! Indeed, all through the previous days the princes and nobles and commoners had marched through the city squares, stopping at churches and calling on God's aid, barefoot and crying, beating their breasts, so grief stricken that father would not greet son, brother would not look at brother. Now you would see them enthusiastically sending out horses, brandishing weapons, and striking their spears. Unable to bear silence in word or deed they celebrated and bantered with one another.

But why do I delay? The order to march went out, and what the princes had decided went according to plan.

Meanwhile, Kerbogah, Duke of the Turks, was playing checkers inside his tent. Hearing the news that the Franks were marching to battle, his thoughts grew troubled, because the report seemed unbelievable. He called to him a Turk by the name of Mirdalin, who had escaped from Antioch, a noble known to us because of his prowess, and he said to him, "What's going on? Didn't you tell me that there were few Franks and that they would never fight against me?"

And Mirdalin answered him, "I never said that they wouldn't fight! But come and I'll look at them and tell you if you will be able to overcome them easily."

At the time the third order of our men was marching out, and when Mirdalin had seen the arrangements of our troops, he said to Kerbogah, "They can be killed, but they cannot be forced to flee."

And Kerbogah said to him, "Can none of them be driven back, even just a little?"

Mirdalin answered, "If the whole pagan nation charged at them, they wouldn't give up so much as a foot of ground."

[3] References to Duke Robert of Normandy, the men of Hugh the Great, and Godfrey of Bouillon and his followers.

Kerbogah was troubled, but he sent many and numerous divisions of men at us, and although up to that time they had kept us from leaving the city, now they allowed us to march peacefully. Our lines turned toward the mountains, lest they encircle us from behind.[4] The mountains, moreover, were about two miles from the bridge. We marched out expansively, as clerics are accustomed to do in religious processions. And this truly was a procession! There were priests and many monks clad in white stoles processing in front of our knights, chanting and invoking the support of God and the patronage of his saints. On the other side, the enemy rushed at us and fired arrows. Kerbogah also sent word to our princes. Now he was ready to make the peace that he had recently refused, so that five or ten Turks might fight against the same number of Franks; whichever knights lost, their side would peacefully cede victory to the other. Our men answered, "You didn't want to do this when we wanted to! Now that we're rushing out to combat, let each one fight for his right!"

Once we had occupied the entire plain, as I have described, some of the Turks stayed behind us and attacked our foot soldiers. The foot soldiers maneuvered around and manfully resisted the enemy's charge. When the Turks could drive them back a little, they set fires around them, so that anyone who did not fear swords might at least shudder before flames. Thus our men had to give ground, because the land was grassy and dry. As our battle lines moved backward, barefoot priests clad in white vestments stood atop the city walls, adjuring God to defend his people and to affirm his covenant, sanctified in his own blood, by granting victory to the Franks in this battle.

Meanwhile, after marching over the lands between the bridge and the mountain, we struggled mightily to keep the enemy from surrounding us as they intended. Their mighty ranks pressed down on us who were in the bishop's cohort, but they couldn't hurt us because of the protection of the Holy Lance, which we carried. I saw everything I'm describing, and I was holding the Holy Lance. But if anyone should say that Heraclius, the vicomte and standard-bearer of the bishop, was wounded in this battle, you should know that he had handed his standard over to someone else and had moved far away from our ranks.[5]

[4] Raymond gives us insight into the basic strategy of the battle lines: Rather than following the other divisions, the Provençals broke toward the mountains to keep the Turks from performing their typical tactic of encircling the army with their cavalry.

[5] In other words, the only person wounded was a man who had ridden out of the lance's protective sphere of power.

When all our men had left the city, five more regiments appeared among us to provide support so that, as it was said, our princes had only established eight divisions, but thirteen contingents left the city.[6]

We should not pass over this one very memorable occurrence. At the beginning of our march, the Lord sent from heaven to his army a light but welcome rain. Whoever felt it was filled with gratitude and strength, and they disparaged the enemy and went forth feeling as if they had been regularly feasting at royal banquets. Its effect was no less miraculous for our horses. Did any horse break down before the battle's end, even if it had not eaten anything for the last eight days except tree leaves and bark? God so multiplied our army that we who had seemed fewer than the enemy before the fight now were in battle far more numerous than they.

Once we had marched out and arranged our lines, we didn't have the chance to engage in the fight before the enemy had turned and fled. Our men pursued them until sunset. The Lord thus worked through his men and their horses. No one left the battle out of greed,[7] and the horses, whose owners had led them to battle with almost no nourishment, fleetly pursued the Turks' swift and well-nourished mounts.

And this was not the only cause for rejoicing that the Lord gave us, for the Turks who had held the citadel against the city, seeing the headlong flight of their fellows, despaired. Some of them surrendered to us with a guarantee that they might live; others fled precipitately. Although this battle was so brutal and frightening, only a few of the enemy knights fell, but hardly any of their foot soldiers escaped. All their tents, moreover, were seized as plunder, along with much gold, silver, and other spoils, such as grain, cattle, and camels without measure or number. Thus we knew again Samaria, where a measure of wheat and barley sold for a shekel.[8]

All this happened on the vigil of the apostles Peter and Paul, at whose intercession our Lord Jesus Christ, who lives and reigns with his servants, through all ages and times, conferred victory upon the pilgrim church of the Franks. Amen.

[6] These were apparently the divisions of saints and martyrs that had been promised in visions during the last month of the siege of Antioch.

[7] In other words, the Franks refrained from plunder until the battle was over.

[8] Not an actual price report; Raymond instead is quoting 2 Kings 7:18, referencing the wars of the Israelites and the Samaritans, as if he and the army were reliving events from the Old Testament.

40

IBN AL-ATHIR

An Arab Historian's Explanation for Kerbogah's Loss

Early Thirteenth Century

Arab historians were as puzzled by Kerbogah's failure as were the Franks, though obviously they did not appeal to miracles or God's will to explain it. Instead, they blamed the loss on the political circumstances of the Turkish world at the end of the eleventh century. Ibn al-Athir once again gives the most succinct summary of Arabic interpretations of the final battle for Antioch.

When Qiwam al-Dawla Karbugha[1] heard of the Franks' doings and their conquest of Antioch, he gathered his forces and marched to Syria. He camped at Marj Dabiq, where the troops of Syria, both Turks and Arabs, rallied to him, apart from those who were in Aleppo. There assembled with him Duqaq ibn Tutush, Tughtakin the Atabeg, Janah al-Dawla the lord of Homs, Arslan Tash the lord of Sinjar, Suqman ibn Artuq and other emirs, the likes of whom are not to be found. Hearing of this, the Franks' misfortunes increased and they were fearful because of their weakness and their shortage of provisions. The Muslims came and besieged them in Antioch, but Karbugha behaved badly towards the Muslims with him. He angered the emirs and lorded it over them, imagining that they would stay with him despite that. However, infuriated by this, they secretly planned to betray him if there should be a battle, and they determined to give him up when the armies clashed.

The Franks, after they had taken Antioch, were left there for twelve days with nothing to eat. The powerful fed on their horses, while the wretched poor ate carrion and leaves. In view of this, they sent to Kar-

[1] A variant spelling of Kerbogah, closer to the Arabic pronunciation.

The Chronicle of Ibn al-Athir for the Crusading Period from al-Kamil fi'l-ta'rikh, trans. D. S. Richards (Surrey, U.K.: Ashgate, 2005), 1:15–17.

bugha, asking him for terms to leave the city, but he did not grant what they sought. He said, "My sword alone will eject you."

The following princes were with them: Baldwin, [Raymond of] St. Gilles, Count Godfrey, the Count lord of Edessa and Bohemond the lord of Antioch, their leader.[2] There was a monk there, of influence amongst them, who was a cunning man. He said to them, "The Messiah (blessings be upon him) had a lance which was buried in the church at Antioch, which was a great building. If you find it, you will prevail, but if you do not find it, then destruction is assured." He had previously buried a lance in a place there and removed the traces [of his digging]. He commanded them to fast and repent, which they did for three days. On the fourth day he took them all into the place, accompanied by the common people and workmen. They dug everywhere and found it as he had said. "Rejoice in your coming victory," he said to them.

On the fifth day they went out of the gate in scattered groups of five or six or so. The Muslims said to Karbugha, "You ought to stand at the gate and kill all that come out, because now, when they are scattered, it is easy to deal with them." He replied, "No, do not do that. Leave them alone until they have all come out and then we can kill them." He did not allow his men to engage them. However, one group of Muslims did kill several that had come out but he came in person and ordered them to desist.

When the Franks had all come out and not one of them remained within, they drew up a great battle line. At that, the Muslims turned their backs in flight, firstly because of the contempt and the scorn with which Karbugha had treated them and secondly because he had prevented them from killing the Franks. Their flight was complete. Not one of them struck a blow with a sword, thrust with a spear, or shot an arrow. The last to flee were Suqman ibn Artuq and Janah al-Dawla because they were stationed in ambush. Karbugha fled with them. When the Franks observed this, they thought that it was a trick, since there had been no battle such as to cause a flight and they feared to pursue them. A company of warriors for the faith stood firm and fought zealously, seeking martyrdom. The Franks slew thousands of them and seized as booty the provisions, money, furnishings, horses and weapons that were in the camp. Their situation was restored and their strength returned.

[2] Baldwin of Edessa, Godfrey's brother, was not at Antioch. Bohemond became lord of Antioch when the city was captured, though his claim to the title was tenuous.

41

RAYMOND OF AGUILERS

The Holy Lance on Trial

ca. 1100

For months after the victory at Antioch, each crusading prince pursued his own particular agenda. It was not until March 14, 1099, that all of the leaders finally rendezvoused at the city of Arqa, with the notable exception of Bohemond, who had decided to stay at Antioch. The different elements of the army were hardly unified, however, their mutual feelings of distrust now coalescing around the Holy Lance of Antioch and Peter Bartholomew, whose visions had grown increasingly subversive. Now he was advocating war not only against Muslims but also against many of the army's own aristocratic leaders. Naturally enough, the targets of Peter's wrath turned against him and demanded that his claims to divine inspiration be put on trial, a series of events and procedures that Raymond of Aguilers describes in great detail, once again appearing to take dictation directly from the visionary.

In the year of the Lord's Incarnation 1099, in the seventh indiction, the twenty-sixth epact, the fifth concurrence, on the nones of April, at night,[1] I, Peter Bartholomew, was lying in the chapel of the Count of Saint-Gilles at the siege of Arqa, thinking about the priest to whom the Lord appeared with his cross when the Turks were besieging us at Antioch.[2] I started to wonder why he had never appeared to me with his cross. Then I saw the Lord enter the chapel, with the apostles Peter and Andrew, and another big, burly dark-skinned man who was nearly bald and had huge eyes.[3] And the Lord said to me, "What are you doing?"

I answered, "Lord, just standing here."

[1] The night of April 5/6, expressed in technically precise liturgical language.
[2] Stephen of Valence, referred to in Document 36.
[3] Probably understood to be St. Paul, traditionally depicted as bald.

Raymond of Aguilers, *Liber*, ed. John H. Hill and Laurita L. Hill (Paris: P. Geuthner, 1969), 112–23. Translated by the author.

And again the Lord said, "You almost drowned with the other people, but what are you thinking about now?"[4]

I answered, "Lord, Father, I was thinking about that priest to whom you appeared with the cross."

And the Lord said, "I knew it!" And then, "Believe that I am the Lord, on whose behalf all of you have come here, and who suffered on the cross at Jerusalem for your sins, as you will now see!"

At that moment I saw a cross there made from two rounded black pieces of wood, unfinished and unformed, except that in the middle the planks were carved so that they could fit together, and the Lord said to me, "Because you wanted the cross—behold! The cross!" And the Lord was stretched out on the cross, crucified, as in the time of the Passion. Peter was holding it up on the right by the head, and Andrew on the left at the neck. The third man was holding it up from the back with his hands.

And the Lord said to me, "Tell these things to my people, that you have seen me in this way. You see my five wounds? In this way, all of you exist in five orders. The first order comprises those who do not fear spears or swords nor any other sort of siege weaponry. That order is similar to me. I came into Jerusalem undeterred by swords and lances, clubs and staffs, and finally the cross. They die for me, and I died for them; I am in them, and they are in me. When people like them die, they are gathered under the right hand of God where, after the resurrection, they will ascend and sit in heaven.

"The second order comprises those who are there to aid the first group and guard their backs, and whom they can turn to for protection. They truly are like the apostles who followed me and dined with me.

"The third order comprises those who provide stones and spears to the second group. They are similar to those who upon seeing me on the cross beat their breasts and bemoaned my injuries.

"The fourth order comprises those who see the surge of battle and hide in their homes and mind their own business, not believing that in my strength there is victory, relying instead on the cleverness of men. They are similar to those who said, 'The penalty is death. Let him be crucified, and he made himself a king and said he was the son of God.'[5]

"The fifth order comprises those who, when they hear the clamor of war while watching from a distance, ask what is causing such a

[4] It is unclear what the drowning incident was.

[5] A conflation of several Gospel passages in which the Jews demand that Pilate crucify Christ.

racket, before offering themselves as examples of cowardice rather than courage, refusing to undergo dangers not only for me but also for their brothers. In the guise of caution, they wish others to fight, or else they provide weapons to warriors, while they themselves are content to watch. They are similar to the traitor Judas and to Pontius Pilate."

He was nude on the cross, covered only with a loin cloth that went to his knees and was of a dull color somewhere between black and red. Around his face were bands of white and red and green. Then, suddenly, the cross was gone, and the Lord was back in the clothes he had been wearing. And I said to him, "Lord God, if I say these things, they won't believe me."

The Lord answered me, "Do you wish to know who doesn't believe you?"

I said, "Yes, Lord."

And the Lord: "The count will gather the princes and the people and instruct them about when the best time would be for a battle or for attacking a castle. The best-known herald will see that the dispositions are carried out after proclaiming three times, 'God help us!' Then you will see the orders form just as I described to you, and you and all the rest who believe will be separated from the unbelievers."

And I said, "What to do about the unbelievers?"

And the Lord answered me, "Don't spare them. Kill them instead, since they are my traitors, brothers of Judas Iscariot. Give their goods to the people in the first order according to need. If you do this, you will locate the straight path that so far you have been wandering around. Just as the other things you have told them have come to pass, so these things will happen, too. Do you know which people I love especially?"

I answered, "The Jewish people."

And the Lord: "Because they were unbelievers, I hate them and hold them to be the least of all peoples. See therefore that you never disbelieve! Otherwise, if you side with the Jews, I will allow another people to accomplish what I have promised to you. Say these things to them: 'Why do you fear to practice justice? What is better than justice?' I want them to cleave to justice. Let them appoint judges from their families and kin groups. Then, when anyone should offend another, let him who suffered the injury say this: 'Brother, would you want this done to you?' Afterward, if the malefactor does not desist, let him accuse him in the name of the authority. Then a judge might legally take all the malefactor's goods. Let half of all the confiscated goods go to the injured party; the rest of the goods will belong to the authority. But if the judge should refuse to take care of this case, go to him and say to him that unless he changes course, he shall not be absolved until the end of the world unless you remit his fault. Do you know how grave a prohibition can be? I forbade Adam to touch the tree of knowledge of good and evil. He transgressed my prohibition, and he and all his descendants were placed in wretched captivity until I came in the flesh and redeemed them by dying on the cross.

"About tithes, some people are doing well, in that they give them as commanded. I will amplify them and make them famous among all the others."

When the Lord had said all this, I began to ask him in the name of charity to restore my ability to read, which he had recently taken from me.[6] And the Lord said, "Isn't what you know enough? Now you want to know more?" And all at once I seemed so wise in my own eyes that I did not ask to know anything further. And the Lord said, "Is what you know enough for you?"

And I answered, "It's enough."

And the Lord spoke again: "What have I said to you? Answer me."

I knew nothing. When he insisted that I repeat to him some of those things that he had said, I answered, "Lord, I've known nothing."

And the Lord said, "Go and tell what you know, and let what you know be enough."[7]

After we had told these things to the brothers, some began to say that they never believed that God would speak to a man of this sort; God would not pass over princes and bishops and show himself to a bumpkin. They even doubted the Lord's Lance. Consequently, we called together the brethren to whom that lance had previously been revealed, and afterward we called on Arnulf, chaplain of the Count of Normandy, who acted as head of all the unbelievers. Because he was learned, many believed him. And we asked him whether he had any doubts. He said that the bishop of Le Puy had doubted it, to which a priest named Peter Desiderius answered:

"I saw the bishop of Le Puy after he had died, and St. Nicholas was with him. We talked about many things, and then the bishop told me this: 'I am in a choir with St. Nicholas, but because I doubted the Lord's Lance, which I ought to have believed in enthusiastically, I was led into hell, where the hair burned off on the right side of my head, and half

[6] Peter Bartholomew had initially claimed to be illiterate, but even his supporters were suspicious, since he seemed familiar with liturgy and scripture.

[7] Raymond now switches back into his own narrative voice.

of my beard burned up, too. Now I am not in pain, but I still will not see God clearly until my hair and beard grow back as they were before.'"

[In support of Peter, Raymond relates a series of visions that members of the army claimed to have experienced. Arnulf seemed to relent and even promised to seek forgiveness for his doubts on an appointed day, but he later requested a reprieve until he had discussed the situation with his lord, Robert of Normandy.]

When Peter Bartholomew heard about this, he was truly furious. Being a simple man who valued truth above all, he said, "I wish and I beg you to make a huge fire, and I will walk through the middle of it with the Lord's Lance. If it is really the Lord's Lance, I will cross through unharmed. If it is not, I will burn up in the fire. For I now see that miracles and visions aren't enough."

We found this to be agreeable and enjoined a fast on him, telling him that the trial by fire would occur four days after the vision, Good Friday, the day the Lord suffered on the cross for our salvation.[8]

As dawn broke, the fire was prepared. After midday, the princes and up to sixty thousand people came together. The priests were there, too, barefoot and clad in white vestments. The fire was made from dried olive branches in two piles, each thirteen feet long and four feet high with about one foot between then. Once the fire was burning fiercely, I, Raymond, said to the multitude: "If Almighty God spoke to this man, face-to-face, and Blessed Andrew showed the Holy Lance to him while he was awake, let him cross through this fire unharmed! If it is a lie, let him burn, along with the lance in his hand!"

Everyone on bended knee answered, "Amen!"

The fire burned intensely. The flames rose thirty cubits into the air. No one could approach it. But Peter, clad only in a tunic, knelt before the bishop of Albara.[9] He then swore with God as his witness that he had seen the Lord face-to-face on the cross and that he had spoken with him and with Blessed Peter and Andrew, as is written above, and that he had invented nothing that he had attributed to Peter, Andrew, and the Lord, and that if he had told any lie at all, he would never cross the fire before him. Whatever he had done against God and his neighbor, he asked God to forgive him, and he asked for the prayers of the bishop,

[8] April 8, 1099.

[9] Peter of Narbonne, appointed to Albara by Raymond of Aguilers after the city was captured in September 1098.

all the priests, and the people who had gathered together to watch the spectacle.

Then the bishop placed the lance into his hands. Peter, still kneeling, made the sign of the cross. The lance in hand, he fearlessly entered the fire. For a time he delayed in the midst of the flames. Then, by the grace of God, he emerged on the other side.

Several people saw a sign: that before he left the pyre, a bird flew over him and dropped down into the burning flames. The priest Evrard . . . saw this, and that best of knights, William the Good, a trustworthy man from the land of Arles, said that he had seen it, too. Another reliable knight from Béziers named William Badboy saw a man wearing a priest's robe (except that he had the garment pulled over his head) enter the fire ahead of Peter, and when he did not see him come out the other side, he began to weep, thinking that Peter Bartholomew was dead, his life extinguished in the flames.

A multitude of people had not been able to see everything that happened. Many other things were revealed to me and were done, but I do not want to write about them for fear of boring readers—especially since three reliable witnesses are enough to prove a case. But this one thing I cannot pass over. After Peter Bartholomew had crossed through the fire, although the flames were burning intensely, the crowd eagerly collected so many brands, coals, and ashes that in a brief time nothing was left of it. In truth, afterward the Lord worked many miracles through them.

As for Peter, he emerged from the flames with neither his tunic nor the thin cloth in which he was carrying the Lord's Lance showing any signs of damage. He held the lance in his hand to show it and shouted loudly, "God help us!" All the people embraced him. Just about the whole multitude of people embraced him, I say, and dragged him around on the ground and trampled him. Everyone hoped to get near him and wanted to touch him and to tear off a bit of his tunic. They opened three or four wounds on his legs, they tore at his flesh, they broke his back, and they kept tossing him around. I think that Peter indeed would have given up the ghost then and there if that strong and most noble knight Raymond Pilet had not broken into that riotous crowd and with a few of his friends rescued Peter at the point of death. But I am so worried and anguished that I can't write further about this.

Raymond Pilet took him to my house. As his wounds were tended to, I started asking him why he had tarried in that fire. He answered, "The Lord approached me in the midst of the flames. Taking me by the hand, he said to me, 'Because you hesitated about looking for the lance after Blessed Andrew had shown it to you, you are not going to cross here unharmed, but you will not see hell.' Having spoken, he sent me forward. Now if you want to, examine my burns."

He did indeed have a few burns around his shins, but not much else. His wounds, however, were extensive. So we called together everyone who had doubted the Lord's Lance, that they might come and examine his face, his head and hair, and all his limbs and so that they might understand whatever he had said about the lance and other things had been true. For he had not feared to enter the flames to prove his words. Many saw him, and saw his face and his whole body, and they praised God, saying, "The Lord can certainly protect us from our enemies' swords given that he freed this man from such an inferno! We don't think that even an arrow could have passed unharmed through the fire that this man crossed."

[Twelve days later, in Raymond's description, Peter died from the wounds incurred after he crossed through the fire, defending to the end the truth of what he had said about the Holy Lance and about everything else he had claimed.]

6

Jerusalem: The Battle for Heaven

42

RALPH OF CAEN

The Armies Arrive at Jerusalem

ca. 1118

The Norman warrior Tancred was now allied with Robert of Normandy as part of the "anti-lance faction." His biographer here reports how Robert's chaplain, Arnulf of Chocques, tried to restore a sense of unity to the army by creating an object of veneration to replace the lance. Ralph then describes how, as the armies approached Jerusalem, Tancred broke away so that he might arrive first and explore the most prophetically charged setting outside Jerusalem's walls: the Mount of Olives.

After the lying fraud Peter suffered his deserved punishment, a meeting was held so that a new source of solace might replace the joy lost when that lance was debunked. An image of the Savior fashioned from the purest gold was offered to the people, on the model of the Israelites' tabernacle. The expense of the former would be as much as the latter, and the devotion of that age might be brought to life again; and the reward, frequent victories over the enemy, was not overlooked. It was declared that thanks must be given to God for the dangers he had eliminated, and prayers needed to be offered for those yet to be faced. Arnulf, the preacher of this message, moved his listeners in whatever direction he

Ralph of Caen, *Gesta Tancredi*, in Recueil des Historiens des Croisades, *Historiens occidentaux* 3 (Paris: Imprimerie Royale, 1866), 683–85. Translated by the author.

wished. The bishop of Martirano, a man little more learned that a commoner, who might be described as a "lettered illiterate," stood nearby so that he might raise his right hand over the people and bless them at the sermon's end. These two assumed the responsibility for making the cross; everybody else helped collect offerings. And so in a brief time this great work was finished, which would have been carried to Jerusalem as a shapeless lump, if the work had not been done with sedulous determination. For as the siege [of Arqa] left the third and entered the fourth month, our princes began to regret their ways. It shamed them that they had put off the road for so long because of an insignificant fortress.

Setting aside useless work, they happily passed by the gates of Tripoli, Jubayl, Beirut, Sidon, Tyre, Acre, Haifa, and Caesarea. From all of these places they boldly demand tribute and abundant supplies, which are freely granted. For all these cities from north to south, in the order described, defended the coast, their tall towers obstructing pilgrims' paths. Finally they put the coast behind them and come to Ramla. Sleepless Tancred moved his camp forward. Before dawn he gathered his companions; he reached Jerusalem; he made a circuit of the wall. (First going to Bethlehem, he freed it from enemies who, besieged, previously had sent a legate asking for help.)[1] At a distance and at first light he saw Jerusalem and made obeisance to it, falling to his knees, eyes turned to the city, his heart in heaven. This poem serves as an image of his emotions:

Praise Jerusalem! Glory of the world.
Whence came our salvation, Christ's Passion,
Ridiculed by shameful Jews,
Bountiful, where humanity's enemy was killed,
As sky, sun, and soil bear witness,
He rescued the guiltless from Orcus.[2]
You[3] suffered the cross, locked in the tomb,
Light from light, goddess born of God,

[1] Tancred did stop at Bethlehem, the birthplace of Christ, on his way to Jerusalem. He would come under some criticism for raising his banner above the Church of the Nativity as if making it his possession.

[2] God of the underworld. This passage describes Christ's harrowing of hell, where he freed the souls of the just who had nonetheless not escaped the punishment of original sin.

[3] The poem addresses Christ here directly.

Entering hell, he led from there
All whom Adam misled, drowned in the Styx.
But he showed that you lived again,
Risen on the third day.
After this he ascended to the ethereal hearth,
For the spotless clouds carried him
Whom the people of Galilee looked up at
And heard, "Thus he will come, as one seeking the stars."
You know these things, holy mount named for olives.
Hail to you, witness to the King's ascent!
Hail again, royal Zion,
Where you pure spirit, you sudden terror
Have filled the disciples with tongues of fire,
As they shout *Kyrie eleison*[4]
In the midst of a sudden sharp noise,
Driven away as if a storm from heaven.
Hail, star of the sea, gates of heaven,
Only mother of the father, daughter of the son,
Ever Virgin during, after, and before
The birth, innocent of the least blemish,
O river running along bending banks,
Fountain, forest, city, hut, mountain, valley, all hail!

When he had planted his banners near the Tower of David[5] and given instructions about setting up camp, he ascended the mountain by himself, alone, without a squire or companion, a great distance away, where he had learned that Christ begotten of God had ascended to the Father. This was either recklessness or a new type of siege—the army of Tancred besieged the west, Tancred alone the east. A few besieged one side; one besieged the other. An army without a leader, a leader without an army, both supported by neither—ay, receiving the help of none! The higher up he went, the further removed he was from the support of the Franks. He was far to the west of those setting camp; the army following was farther west still.

Equal parts knight, foot soldier, and standard-bearer, Tancred directed his gaze from the Mount of Olives to the city, separated only by the gash through the landscape that is the Valley of Jehoshaphat. He

[4] "Lord have mercy." A Greek expression also used in the Latin liturgy.
[5] Traditional name for the tower at the western gate of Jerusalem.

looked at the people hurrying about, the fortified towers, the rumbling army, the men rushing to arms, the young women bursting into tears, the priests turned to prayers, filling the byways with a shriek, a shout, a peal, a bray. He marveled at the ethereal dome of the Temple of the Lord, at the unheard-of length of the Temple of Solomon, the curving of its grand arcade like another city within the city.[6] But repeatedly his eyes went back to Mount Calvary and the Temple of the Holy Sepulcher. At a great distance, the sites were nonetheless laid out before him because of the exertions he had made to reach higher ground. Crying over these sights, abasing himself before them, he longed to exchange his life for the light, if only he might be permitted to kiss the footsteps of Calvary, whose he heights he now observed.

[6]Tancred thus regarded the Temple Mount and marveled, respectively, at the Dome of the Rock and al-Aqsa Mosque.

43

An Imagined Battle outside the Holy City

1250

This image, from a 1250 illustrated copy of the book of Revelation (a genre of manuscript that became extremely popular in the years following the crusade), depicts a battle between the forces of Christ and Antichrist fought outside the holy city.

Kharbine-Tapabor / The Art Archive at Art Resource, N.Y.

44

RAYMOND OF AGUILERS

The Main Army Arrives at Jerusalem

ca. 1100

Raymond of Aguilers recounts how the rest of the army arrived at Jerusalem. The tone and content of his account differ from those of Ralph of Caen's in Document 42.

Leaving a garrison and a new bishop in the camp at Ramla, we loaded up our camels and oxen and all our beasts of burden and turned our path toward Jerusalem. We forgot or else discounted the orders Peter Bartholomew had given us, that we shouldn't approach Jerusalem unless we took our shoes off two leagues away. Each man instead wished to get ahead of the other out of ambition to occupy castles and villages. It was now customary among us that whoever got to a castle or village first could put his banner over it without anyone challenging his possession of it. They were getting up in the middle of the night because of this ambition, not waiting for their companions, and capturing all the mountains and villages on the plains of the Jordan. A few were more concerned about God's commandment and went barefoot, sighing heavily about the contempt shown toward God's word. But no one was able to convince a companion or friend to leave the path of ambition. When finally in this arrogant fashion we had come near to Jerusalem, the Jerusalemites came out and met the first of our men and gravely harmed our horses. Three or four died, and many were wounded.

Raymond of Aguilers, *Liber*, ed. John H. Hill and Laurita L. Hill (Paris: P. Geuthner, 1969), 137. Translated by the author.

45

ALBERT OF AACHEN

The Procession before the Final Battle

ca. 1107

After one failed attack, the crusaders set about making careful siege preparations, eventually setting July 14, 1099, as the target date for their final assault. Their arrival at Jerusalem had not overcome the fundamental divisions within the army. If the attack were to be successful—or, put another way, if an angry God were to be appeased—the crusaders needed to make one last propitiatory gesture toward heaven. On July 8, therefore, all of the soldiers set aside their disagreements to participate in a grand religious procession. Albert of Aachen, though not himself a crusader, was able to draw remarkably detailed information from his sources about this stage of the expedition.

As the affliction of thirst grew worse and as the Catholic people continued to struggle in the siege, it seemed to the nobles, based on the advice of the bishops and the clergy who were on hand, that they ought to seek advice from a certain man of God who lived as a hermit in an ancient tower near the summit of the Mount of Olives. They should inquire what to do and what should be their priority, and they should tell him how they burned with a desire to enter the city and to see the Lord's sepulcher and how many dangers they had survived on the road because of their faith and because of the vow they had taken. When the man of God learned about their plans and their desire, he offered them advice, saying that first they ought to embrace a regime of painful fasting and of continual prayers of devotion. After this program, with God's aid, they could safely assault the city walls and the Saracens.

Now, based on the man of God's counsel, the bishops and the clergy ordered a three-day fast, and on Friday all the Christians made a procession around the city, coming first to the Mount of Olives and the place where Lord Jesus ascended to heaven and then going to another

---

Albert of Aachen, *Historia Ierosolimitana, History of the Journey to Jerusalem*, ed. and trans. Susan B. Edgington (Oxford: Clarendon Press, 2007), 412–14. Translated by the author.

place where he taught his disciples how to pray the Lord's Prayer, and they stood there in humility and devotion. In that same place on the mountain, Peter the Hermit and a cleric of great learning and charisma named Arnulf of Chocques (a castle in Flanders) gave a sermon to the people, and they put to rest much of the discord that for diverse reasons had grown among the pilgrims. In particular, they settled the dispute between Count Raymond and Tancred over a payment of money that the count had unjustly withheld from Tancred. Because of spiritual admonitions, the princes' hearts softened and a loving concord returned. That quarrel was settled and many other Christian brothers similarly entered back into accord. Thus the whole procession of Christians descended from the aforementioned place on the Mount of Olives and went to nearby Mount Zion and into the church of the holy mother of God.

There the clergy, clad in white vestments and reverently carrying saints' relics, and many of the best laymen were hit by arrows from Saracens patrolling the walls and keeping watch over them. The city was indeed one arrow's length from this church on Zion. In this same place to further provoke Christians to rage, Saracens subjected crucifixes to ridicule and shame. They spat on them and did not even refrain from urinating on them in the sight of all.

46

BAUDRY OF BOURGUEIL

An Imagined Sermon Delivered to Crusaders at Jerusalem

1107

Like Urban II's sermon at Clermont, we cannot know exactly what the preachers in these processions said to the troops. The monastic chronicler Baudry of Bourgueil, writing in 1107, imagined one of the preachers arguing that the crusade was not merely a battle for an earthly city but also a war with otherworldly implications. An educated and urbane

Baudry of Bourgueil, *Historia Hierosolymitana,* in Recueil des Historiens des Croisades, *Historiens occidentaux* 4 (Paris: Imprimerie Royale, 1879), 100–101. Translated by the author.

observer known as much for his romantic poetry as for his historical writing, Baudry was probably providing not an accurate report of a sermon preached on that day but, rather, a summation, from his perspective, of what the crusade had been all about.

Before they attacked the city, the bishops and priests, clad in ecclesiastical vestments, addressed the people, and one in particular set himself up on a higher place and spun his words in this way:

Listen, brothers and lords! Although you already know all the things that I am about to tell you—you've heard them many times now!—still it is beautiful and sweet and pleasurable to preach anew about the Lord our God. It always behooves you to hear and to understand. In this city, right in front of us, Christ redeemed you. In this city God established Christianity. From this city emanated to us the sacrament of Christianity. From our lands we came here so that we might pray before and kiss the sepulcher of our God. This city, which you now see, is the cause of all our labor. This city is the image of heavenly Jerusalem. It is the form of that other city for which we long.[1]

Do you see with what determination a senseless, lowly, and utterly alien people hold this city against us? Do you see with what stubbornness they possess what ought to be ours and what is not rightfully theirs? You know with what gall they have defiled God's sanctuary. You know how they have left the holy city downtrodden underneath their noxious crimes. But let's consider this carefully and properly. This Jerusalem you see, which you have attained, before which you stand, prefigures and denotes the heavenly city. Our visible enemies hold this city against us, just as invisible enemies against whom spiritual warfare is necessary block the paths leading to heaven. How much more difficult is it to fight against spiritual wickedness in the heavens than against the flesh-and-blood enemies whom we now see? The enemies mocking us in the city are limbs of those other enemies,[2] lesser and weaker versions of their masters. But if these enemies, who are almost nothing, can conquer us and keep from us the city that we now see, what do you think their lords will do if their servants dare such deeds?

Be sure of this: We must fear that the heavenly city will be closed to us, will be taken away from us, if evil enemies disinherit us from our

[1]The language comes from Eucharistic theology: Jerusalem is the "form" of heaven, just as the bread and wine are the external image, or form, of Christ's body and blood.

[2]Demons.

home while we sit idly by. We will prove impotent and ineffectual in spiritual combat if we are unable to bark back against these dull, weak, and effeminate dogs, if we do not deliberately answer them death for death.

Arise, then, family of Christ! Arise and be at the ready, knights and foot soldiers! Lay claim now to this city, our commonwealth![3] And think on Christ, who until today has been outlawed and crucified in this city. With Joseph,[4] take him from the cross and bury him, an incomparably desirable treasure, within the sepulcher of your heart. Manfully set him free from the wicked men who crucify him. As often as the corrupt judges, accomplices of Herod and Pilate, mock and bedevil your brothers, they also crucify Christ. As often as they torment and kill your brothers, they strike Christ's side again with the Lance of Longinus! They do all this, and what is worse, they ridicule and mock our law and deliberately antagonize us with their impudent words.

What are you to do? Is it right for you to see and hear these things and not to weep? I say this to you, fathers and sons, brothers and nephews: If an outsider struck one of your kin, would you not avenge your own blood? How much more ought you avenge your God, your father, your brother, whom you now see ridiculed by outlaws, crucified, whom you hear crying, despairing, and begging for help? *I have trodden the winepress alone, and no man from the nations is with me.*[5]

Get to it! Arm yourselves with confidence! Attack this city as God's auxiliaries! To die on behalf of Christ in this place will be something beautiful for you, on whose behalf Christ died in this city. March now to battle! Your leader will support you in battle and reward your good intentions and glorious deeds!

[3]Baudry's term here is *res publica*, the term used for the republic in Rome.

[4]According to the Gospel, Joseph of Arimathea donated his tomb for the burial of Christ.

[5]Isaiah 63:3. Like other writers, Baudry suggests here that the crusade was foretold by the prophets of the Old Testament. The image of the winepress also recalls New Testament prophecy, specifically Revelation 14:20, cited in Document 47.

47

RAYMOND OF AGUILERS

The Battle for Jerusalem

ca. 1100

Once the crusaders had broken through Jerusalem's walls, they transformed the city into a scene out of the book of Revelation—for Raymond of Aguilers, literally so.

The onset of night doubled everyone's fears.[1] The Saracens feared that our men might take the city in darkness, or on the following day, the inner wall might be swiftly captured, now that the curtain wall had been taken and a trench filled. By contrast our men were afraid that the Saracens might take comfort in setting our siege works on fire, now that they were close to the city. As a result each side kept watch, worked hard, and struggled to stay awake. On one side was sure hope; on the other, doubtful fear. This side worked willingly to capture the city for their God; the other side under compulsion resisted because of Muhammad's laws. The many great works undertaken by each army during the night are a wonder to believe.

The next morning, our men burned with desire to reach the walls, and they moved their siege towers into place. The Saracens had also constructed siege machinery so that against every one of ours they might oppose nine or ten of theirs. As a result they hindered our efforts. It was, however, the ninth day—the day on which the priest said that the city would be taken.[2]

[1] July 14, 1099, after the first day of the attack had ended.

[2] Nine days earlier, the priest Peter Desiderius (who was mentioned in Document 41) had informed the army that Bishop Adhémar's ghost had told him when the city would fall.

Raymond of Aguilers, *Liber*, ed. John H. Hill and Laurita L. Hill (Paris: P. Geuthner, 1969), 148–51. Translated by the author.

But why am I delaying? Our siege towers[3] were collapsing under catapults' bombardment, and our men were failing because of sheer exhaustion. Yet the mercy of God—invincible, unconquerable, present in every tribulation—was there with them. I can't pass over this one detail. As two women tried to hex one of our catapults, a stone from the same machine manfully struck them as they chanted and killed them, along with three girls. Thus we cut off their incantations while extracting their souls!

Around midday, our men were troubled by exhaustion and despair. There were many on the enemy side to oppose each of us, and the wall was as tall and solid as ever, giving the defenders the means to oppose us. As we wearied and they celebrated, God's mediating mercy arrived and turned our sadness into a joy unfelt for many days. At that moment some men were trying to decide whether to withdraw our siege machinery, which had been partly burned, partly crushed. But then a knight on the Mount of Olives began to wave his shield at those of us following the count and to others, signaling us to go forward. Who this knight was I never learned. Our exhausted men took comfort in this signal and once more approached the walls, some with ladders and some tossing up ropes.

Also, a young man had set afire his arrows, which he had prepared with cotton padding, and aimed them at the rampart the Saracens were using against the wooden siege tower of the duke and the two counts.[4] The first caught, and its flames drove away the men who had been defending that fortification. The duke and his men swiftly lowered a wickerwork wall that had been defending the top of the tower and thus made a bridge. Bravely and fearlessly, they entered Jerusalem. Among the first to cross were Tancred and the Duke of Lotharingia. Together they spilled so much blood that day that it seems hardly credible. After them, all the others climbed onto the walls, and the Saracens now suffered.

But let me tell you something amazing. Although the Franks had almost taken the city, the ones fighting the count continued to resist as if nothing had happened. But once our men had captured city walls and towers, then you would have seen marvels! Some were decapitated,

[3]Wooden towers built to be taller than the city walls. Archers perched at the top of the towers would try to provide cover for warriors on the ground to approach, undermine, and perhaps break through the walls.

[4]Duke Godfrey, Robert of Flanders, and Robert of Normandy. Without any narrative indication, Raymond has confusingly shifted his description to the opposite side of Jerusalem.

which was fortunate for them. Others, riddled with arrows, tried to jump off the towers. Still others caught on fire and suffered and burned for a long, long time. You would have seen in the city streets and squares piles of heads and hands and feet. Corpses were everywhere along the paths of men and horses. But these points are trivial. Let me tell you about the Temple of Solomon, where they used to perform their rites and ceremonies. What happened there? If I tell you the truth, you won't believe it. Let it suffice to say that in the Temple and Portico of Solomon, knights were riding up to their knees in blood and that the blood reached the horses' bridles.[5] And it was only fair that that place should receive the blood of people whose blasphemies against God it had so long endured. Corpses and blood filled the city. Many fled to the Tower of David and asked for a pledge of safety from Count Raymond, and they handed the citadel over to him.

The reward for the capture of the city was to see the devotion of pilgrims before the Lord's Sepulcher. How they clapped their hands, rejoiced, and sang a new song to the Lord.[6] Their thoughts presented to the victorious and triumphant God a covenant of praise, which words cannot describe.

A new day, a new joy, new and endless happiness, the culmination of our labor and devotion, new words, a new song never ending from all the people! This day, I say, will forever be celebrated! It turned all our suffering and labor into joy and rejoicing! This day, I say, was the destruction of all paganism, the proof of Christianity, and the renewal of our faith. *This is the day that the Lord has made. We will rejoice and be glad in it!*[7] And rightly so, since the Lord illumined and blessed his people on this day. On this day many people saw Lord Adhémar, Bishop of Le Puy, in the city. In fact, many swore that he was the first person who climbed the wall, and that he called his companions and the people to climb up after him.

[5]Revelation 14:20.

[6]A reference to Psalms 96:1, with Raymond again identifying the crusaders with the Old Testament armies of Israel.

[7]Psalms 118:24.

48

RALPH OF CAEN

Tancred Confronts Antichrist

1118

In the midst of the battle, Tancred attacked the Dome of the Rock and stripped it of its wealth. Inside he found a large silver sculpture (probably the elaborate candelabrum mentioned by Ibn al-Athir in Document 49), which he took to be a statue of Muhammad. Tancred in turn believed Muhammad to be a precursor of Antichrist. Ralph of Caen possibly heard this story from Tancred himself.

But Tancred the man was not man, but a lion—a lion who does not have the mouth of a lion, but rather the heart of a lion, raging toward greater heights.[1] What neither Ajax would dream nor Hector and the Hectorean conqueror Achilles could dare, this descendant of the Guiscardian duke did easily and without thought.[2] In the court of the temples (now one, previously two, now only of the Lord, previously of the Lord and Solomon), this one has a curving wall; that one faced south.[3] It is grand and spacious and surrounded with high walls; barred with a double entryway, it had welcomed flight and fear, horror and war, which is to say, the whole city. This entryway was firm and inflexible, made of iron, but Tancred, harder than iron, beat at it, broke it, wore it down, and entered. At his entry the crowd cannot escape. They burst into Solomon's five-sided courtyard. The slow fall before his sword; the swift flee from his sword. Fleeing together, they shut the door and bolt the latch, either in hopes of saving their lives or at least of postponing death. But the victor turns

[1]This passage is entirely in verse in the original Latin.

[2]A reference to Robert Guiscard, Bohemond's father.

[3]Ralph seems to be drawing comparisons between the modern temple complex, which included (and includes) the Dome of the Rock and al-Aqsa Mosque, and the biblical Temple of Solomon.

Ralph of Caen, *Gesta Tancredi*, in Recueil des Historiens des Croisades, *Historiens occidentaux* 3 (Paris: Imprimerie Royale, 1866), 695–96.[1] Translated by the author.

to the temple of the Lord, and voila! The doors open before his standard, the heights to his flag.

A tall idol cast from heavy silver was standing high on a pedestal, which six strong men could hardly move and ten could hardly lift. When Tancred looks at this, he says, "O for shame! What does it want, this idol here standing so tall? What does this effigy want? Why is it covered in gems, gold, purple cloth?" For Mahummet had been clad all over in gems and purple cloth, and he shone with gold. "Perhaps this is an image of Mars or Apollo? Surely it is not Christ? No, there are no markers of Christ here—no cross, no wreath, no nails, no pierced side. Therefore this is not Christ, but rather the first Antichrist. Wicked Mahummet! Evil Mahummet! If only his companion were here now, the one to come! At this moment my feet would stomp on both Antichrists. O for shame! The society of hell has attained the tower of God, and the slave of Pluto has become a god in the edifice of Solomon! Let him fall now just as that other one has long since fallen![4] Will he stand proud as if he has swallowed us whole?"

The order had hardly been given before you would have seen it carried out. The knights follow no command more gladly than this one. They take it down, drag it out, break it apart, shatter it. The material is precious, but the shape is vile metal. Thus something precious was crafted out of something vile.

[4]Since Muslims have never worshipped idols, it is unclear what Tancred saw or imagined he saw. In any case, he seems to suggest that Muhammad was the first Antichrist and will come again, on the model of how Christ is expected to return. It is not a theologically sound model but might reflect how a warrior would grasp prophetic ideas. Referring to Muhammad as "the son of Pluto" allows Ralph to suggest that Muhammad is both a pagan God and spawned from the underworld.

49

IBN AL-ATHIR

An Arab Historian on the Fall of Jerusalem

Early Thirteenth Century

Ibn al-Athir gives a much more succinct description of the battle, which is nonetheless packed with detail and can be compared to Documents 47 and 48.

The Egyptians appointed as deputy in Jerusalem a man called Iftikhar al-Dawla, who remained there until this present time, when the Franks attacked after they had besieged Acre but with no success. After their arrival they erected forty trebuchets or more and they constructed two towers, one on the Mount Zion side, but the Muslims burnt that one and killed all inside. After they had completely destroyed it by fire, their help was then called for, as the city defences had been overwhelmed on the other side. The Franks did indeed take the city from the north in the forenoon of Friday, seven days remaining of Sha'ban. The inhabitants became prey for the sword. For a week the Franks continued to slaughter the Muslims. A group of Muslims took refuge in the Tower of David and defended themselves there. They resisted for three days and then the Franks offered them safe-conduct, so they surrendered the place. The Franks kept faith with them and they departed at night for Ascalon, where they remained.

In the Aqsa Mosque the Franks killed more than 70,000,[1] a large number of them being imams, ulema,[2] righteous men and ascetics. Muslims who had left their native lands and come to live a holy life in this august spot. The Franks took forty or more silver candlesticks from the

[1]An exaggeration, but probably an attempt to convey how tremendous the death toll seemed.

[2]An imam is a leader in a mosque; an ulema is a Muslim legal scholar.

The Chronicle of Ibn al-Athir for the Crusading Period from al-Kamil fi'l-ta'rikh, trans. D. S. Richards (Surrey U.K.: Ashgate, 2005), 1:21–22.

Dome of the Rock, each of which weighed 3,600 dirhams, and also a silver candelabrum weighing forty Syrian rotls. They removed 150 small candlesticks of silver and twenty or so of gold. The booty they took was beyond counting.

50

ALBERT OF AACHEN

The Treatment of Prisoners

ca. 1107

The capture of Jerusalem would have seemed extraordinarily brutal to Latin Christian warriors, who before the crusade were accustomed to conflict on a fairly small scale. But despite the ruthless conquest of July 15, 1099, many of Jerusalem's Muslim citizens did survive. Tancred took a group of them hostage on the Temple Mount, hoping to collect ransoms to add to his share of plunder. Raymond of Saint-Gilles was holding another group of hostages in the Tower of David (a group referred to in Document 49 above), who did manage to ransom themselves and escape. Still other Muslims seemed to survive simply by hiding. Albert of Aachen describes the fate of these men, women, and children on July 17, in some detail. His recounting of these events is unique among Latin Christian writers. Perhaps he was again drawing on his unusually rich collection of eyewitness testimony.

Count Raymond, corrupted by greed, accepted a great ransom for Saracen knights whom he had trapped after they had fled into the Tower of David, and he allowed them to leave unharmed. All their weapons, food, and valuables he kept along with the tower. As the Sabbath dawned the next day, about three hundred Saracens had escaped our weapons and taken refuge on the roof of the glorious house of Solomon, hoping for

Albert of Aachen, *Historia Ierosolimitana, History of the Journey to Jerusalem,* ed. and trans. Susan B. Edgington (Oxford: Clarendon Press, 2007), 438–42. Translated by the author.

survival. In danger of death, they begged and pled for their lives, trusting no one's pledge or promise until they had received Tancred's standard as a token of protection and life. But it did those miserable people little good. For many Christians were upset and moved to anger over this arrangement, and not one of the Saracens escaped alive.

The glorious knight Tancred felt a burning fury over this affront to him, and vengeance alone would have calmed his wrath if the counsel and judgment of greater and wiser men had not mollified his thoughts in this fashion: "Jerusalem, the city of God in heaven, has today, as all of you know, been restored to his own children, recovered with great difficulty and not without significant losses on our side—freed from the hand of the King of Babylon and Turkish tyranny. But now we have to be careful lest we spare our captives and the other gentiles here and thus lose the city through avarice or sloth or mercy to the enemy. For if by chance the King of Babylon besieges us with a great army, we will have to fight both internal and external enemies, resulting in our perpetual exile. Whence the best and truest counsel seems to us to cut down with the sword right away all the Saracens and gentiles whom we are holding captive in hopes of ransom or for whom we have received ransom. Otherwise, their deceit and cunning might lead us into further difficulties.

They agreed to this plan and on the third day after the victory, the leaders sent out a decree, and behold! Everyone took up arms and inflicted a wretched destruction on the remaining collection of gentiles. Some they led out in chains and decapitated. Others whom they had previously spared for money or out of simple decency they found in the city streets and squares and butchered. Girls, women, noble ladies, pregnant women, and women with little children they decapitated or stoned to death, giving no consideration to age. For their part, the girls, women, and noble ladies, horror-struck and terrified of sudden death, clutched at the Christians and begged for their lives, even as the Christians gleefully and savagely slashed open the throats of men and women. Some of the women embraced their feet and with miserable tears and sobs entreated them for their lives. Boys five or three years old, seeing the cruel fates of their mothers and fathers, together wept and shouted in misery. But these gestures toward piety and mercy were in vain. For the Christians had so wholly given their thoughts to slaughter that a nursing boy or a girl or a babe not yet a year old could not escape the hand of the persecutor. The streets of the whole city of Jerusalem were littered and covered with the dead, dismembered bodies of men and women. Not only in the streets, homes, and palaces, but even in places of seclusion piles of corpses were everywhere found.

51

Christ Leads Crusading Knights into Armageddon

Early Fourteenth Century

This image, taken from an early-fourteenth-century illustrated commentary of the book of Revelation, depicts Christ as a rider on a white horse, leading crusading knights into the last battle between good and evil at the end of history, as described in Revelation 19. It demonstrates the enduring imaginative connections between crusading, prophecy, and holy war.

7

Aftermath

52

ARCHBISHOP MANASSES OF REIMS

Latin Christian Reaction to the Crusade

1099

In late 1099, Archbishop Manasses of Reims wrote a letter celebrating the crusade to Bishop Lambert of Arras—the same man who attended the Council of Clermont in 1095 and recorded the text of the crusade indulgence quoted in Document 15. The public celebrations that Manasses ordered help explain how news of the crusaders' victory spread as quickly as it did. The letter also touches on prophetic themes in its depiction of the earthly and heavenly Jerusalems and gives evidence of how the idea of crusader martyrdom was understood among churchmen at the end of the expedition.

Manasses, by the grace of God Archbishop of Reims, to Lambert his confrère, Bishop of Arras, greetings in Christ Jesus.

Let it be known to you, dearest brother, that a true and joyful rumor has recently come to our ears, and we believe it to have happened not through human power but by divine majesty: Jerusalem is fixed joyfully and happily in heaven. Jerusalem, city and glory of our redemption, rejoices with unexpected joy! For through the toil and incomparable might of the sons of God she is delivered from cruelest pagan slavery.

Heinrich Hagenmeyer, *Die Kreuzzugsbriefe aus den Jahren 1088–1100* (Hildesheim: Georg Olms, 1901), ep. 20, 175–76. Translated by the author.

We rejoice—we whose belief in Christianity in these times is placed in a glass of eternal clarity![1]

Summoned, called, and compelled not only by letters sent from our lord Pope Paschal, but also by the humble prayers of Duke Godfrey, whom the Christian army by divine ordinance has raised up as king, and also by the honeyed appeal of Lord Arnulf, whom the army unanimously raised to the patriarchal see, we now write to you with a similar charity so that you might cause prayers to be said continually in all your parish churches, along with fasts and acts of charity, so that the King of Kings and Lord of Lords might bring victory to King Godfrey against the enemies of Christians and so that he might grant faith and wisdom to the patriarch against heretical sects.[2] We equally command and enjoin you in the name of obedience to constrain with threats everyone who vowed to undertake this expedition and took the sign of the cross to proceed to Jerusalem and aid their brothers—provided they are sufficiently healthy and have the means to complete the journey. As for the rest, skillfully, devotedly, and continually urge them through your sermons never to neglect the assistance due to the people of God, so that the first and the last shall equally receive the denarius promised to laborers in the vineyard.[3] Farewell!

Pray for the bishop of Le Puy, the bishop of Orange, Anselm of Ribemont,[4] and all the others who attained a glorious martyrdom and died in peace.

[1] A play on Paul's famous dictum that we now see "through a glass darkly" (1 Corinthians 13:12).

[2] Presumably, Manasses is hoping for the conversion of Eastern Christians.

[3] Matthew 20:1–6. This is one of Christ's parables, where vineyard workers receive the same wage regardless of the number of hours worked. In this context, crusaders who departed in 1100 would receive the same reward as those who left in 1096.

[4] The knight Anselm of Ribemont had written two letters to Manasses before his death on crusade. Of the three crusaders mentioned here, only Anselm died in combat. Bishops Adhémar of Le Puy and William of Orange seem to have died of illnesses.

53

ALI IBN TAHIR AL-SULAMI

Muslim Reaction to the Crusade

1105

The first Arab writer we have who seems to have understood the crusade in terms of holy war was Ali ibn Tahir al-Sulami. His 1105 treatise calling for a unified Muslim response to the crusaders' aggression in the Middle East, however, would go more or less unheeded for the next seventy-five years.

In the name of God, the just and merciful!

The apostle of Allah says, "The caliphate pertains to the Quraysh, authority to the Ansari, the call to Islam to the Abyssinians, and the *hijra* and *jihad* henceforth pertain to Muslims."[1] The statement that jihad henceforth pertains to Muslims proves that the duty falls on all Muslims, and if it falls on all of them, it will do so until the day of Resurrection.

Abu Muhammad Sunayd b. Da'ud at-Tartusi says in his *Book of Commentary*, "Makhul turned toward the *qibla* and made ten oaths that warfare is an obligation," adding, "If it pleased you, you could do more."

In terms of general consensus, the first four caliphs, also companions of the Prophet, agreed after the Prophet's death that jihad is the duty of all. In effect, none of the four neglected it during his reign, and the caliphs after them continued to follow that model. Every year the ruler personally led attacks against the lands of unbelievers or else charged someone to lead the attacks in his place. Such was the practice until one of the caliphs neglected this duty out of weakness. His successors

[1]The Quraysh were Muhammad's tribe in Mecca; the Ansari were Muhammad's allies in Mecca; the *hijra* is Muhammad's journey from Mecca to Medina, year 1 of the Islamic calendar. The intent of the sentence is to stress that jihad is the duty of all Muslims and not of any particular group.

Emmanuel Sivan, "La genèse de la contre-croisade: Un traité damasquin du début du XIIe siècle," *Journal Asiatique* 254 (1966): 214–22. This translation is based on Sivan's French translation.

did the same, for the same reason or else for similar ones. This suspension of jihad—worsened by the failure of Muslims to carry out other obligations of the law as well as their violations of certain legal prohibitions—resulted inevitably in God pitting the Muslims against one another. Enmity and hatred grew among them, and their enemies felt a new desire to drive them from their lands and thus assuage their own greed. One group of unbelievers made a surprise attack on Sicily, profiting from the divisions and rivalries that prevailed there. In the same way unbelievers have captured city after city in Spain.[2] When they heard rumors of the disturbances in this country,[3] where rulers hated each other and battled one another, they resolved to invade. And Jerusalem was the target of their desire.

In Syria, they saw the states at odds with one another, separated in their beliefs and their relations undermined by an unceasing desire for vengeance. The unbelievers' greed grew strong and reinforced their determination to attack. In fact, they zealously practiced jihad against Muslims, who for their part brought only listlessness and disunity to war, each striving to leave this duty to others. Thus the unbelievers successfully conquered lands far greater than they had intended, massacring and humiliating the local population. At this very moment they are striving to increase their conquests. Their greed knows no limits because of the torpid opposition they have met from men content to live free of danger. Now they expect confidently to become masters over the whole country and make prisoners of all who live here. Their wishes are nearly fulfilled.

Al-Shafi'i says:[4] "The minimal obligation on the leader of the community is to make one incursion a year into the lands of the unbelievers, led either by himself or by his troops, in the name of Islam and after the fashion of jihad. It must happen every year, except in unusual circumstances." He adds, "If not enough troops are mobilized to carry out the attack in a satisfactory manner, then the duty of fighting the unbelievers falls on everyone left behind, following the command of God the most high." Thus he demonstrates that in case of necessity, jihad becomes a personal obligation, as is the case now, when these troops unexpectedly attack Muslim lands.

[2] A reference to eleventh-century wars in Italy and Spain that preceded the First Crusade.

[3] Syria.

[4] A ninth-century Muslim jurist.

Al-Ghazali says:[5] "Each year that a raid was not organized, all Muslims who were free, responsible for their own actions, and able to carry arms went out in sufficient numbers to make war against the enemy. Their goal was to exalt the word of God; to make their religion triumph over their enemies, the polytheists;[6] to win the heavenly reward that God and his apostle promised to anyone who fights on behalf of God; and to plunder the wealth, the women, and the property of the unbelievers." The reason is that jihad is a collective duty, such that a community that borders the enemy can by itself make war against unbelievers and thus keep at bay the danger. But if a frontier community is too weak to hold the enemy in check, then the duty to help falls on the neighboring country—in this case, Syria. If the enemy attacks a Syrian city that is unable to resist it, then all the cities in Syria must raise an army capable of opposition. Other countries are exempted because the cities of Syria together can be considered as essentially a single city. But if all the warriors in Syria are not enough for the task, then the inhabitants of neighboring countries are duty-bound to help, in a perimeter large enough to drive out the enemy. The countries further removed are exempted from this duty. . . .

Devote yourself to the duty of jihad! Help one another to protect your religion and your brothers! Seize the opportunity to invade the unbelievers' lands. It will not require great effort, and God has prepared you for it. It is a paradise that God brings near to you, a good that you may readily acquire in this world, a glory that will last for many years. Do not lose this opportunity; otherwise, God may condemn you in the next life to suffer the fires of hell.

Your doubts dissolved, you must now feel sure of your personal obligation to wage war for the faith. This burden falls especially on the sultan to whom God has entrusted his subjects' fates, in that he must care for their needs and defend Muslim lands. It is absolutely essential that the sultan each year attack the lands of the unbelievers and chase them from them and that he enjoin upon the emirs henceforth to exalt the word of the faith and to discredit that of the unfaithful. In this way he might discourage the enemies of God's religion from undertaking anew such military campaigns. It is astonishing to think how sultans continue to lead lives of ease and tranquillity in the face of this ongoing catastrophe—to wit, the unbelievers' conquest of their country, the

[5]A Persian jurist and philosopher and a contemporary of al-Sulami.

[6]Muslims often refer to Christians as polytheists because of their veneration for the Trinity, an incomprehensible doctrine to adherents of strict monotheism.

forced deportation of some, and the lives of humiliation imposed upon others, with everything that entails, including slaughter, imprisonment, and continual suffering day and night.

In the name of God, O sultans of this country and of you who obey them, brave soldiers and warriors, property owners great and small, "Go forth, with light or heavy arms, and strive with your goods and your lives for the cause of God!" "O you who believe, if you help God, He will help you and firmly plant your feet."[7] Do not quarrel with one another, for fear that you will suffer defeat and your troops will be decimated. Have faith in the divine struggle, and you will be raised above your enemies. Strive to drive fear from your hearts; be assured that your religion, even if it is sometimes touched with weakness, will endure according to the promise of God until the Last Judgment. Never lend an ear to the words of his enemies, apostates, worshippers of the stars, and astrologers. Know well that God has sent this enemy against you only to punish and to test you, as is read in his book: "We will test you to know among you those who strive to the best of their abilities and who are steadfast, and we will test what is said of you."[8]

Similarly, you must learn that the Prophet promised victory over the enemy to a group within his community, naming especially the inhabitants of Syria. Perhaps it is you whom he designated? The Apostle of God[9] also said, "Part of my community will never cease to fight and to triumph in the cause of the true religion until the End of Days; no desertion can harm them." According to one tradition, which seems to me to have a reliable chain of citations, these troops are Syrians. According to another tradition, the struggle will concern the inhabitants of Jerusalem and the surrounding area.

And here is the proof that Jerusalem is going to return to the hands of Islam and that a community of believers, whose inhabitants will have these characteristics, will establish themselves in Jerusalem until the Last Days. This tradition is authentic:

We have heard a hadith[10] from a reliable chain of transmission that says that the Byzantines will take Jerusalem for a predetermined period and that the Muslims will assemble against them, chase them from that city, and kill most of them. Then they will pursue the survivors on the road back to Constantinople, which they will besiege and conquer. This

[7]Qur'an 9:41 and 47:7.
[8]Qur'an 47:31.
[9]Muhammad.
[10]A saying attributed to the Prophet Muhammad or a story about him outside the Qur'an.

hadith is certain. If so, it clearly follows that the community that will fight and triumph for the faith is the same one that, thanks to heavenly assistance, will drive the unbelievers from Jerusalem and from other Muslim territories—the same one that will also capture Constantinople.[11] Apply yourself, then, to this holy war. It is just possible that you are the ones destined to win the prize of that great conquest, the ones chosen for this noble distinction.

[11]The implication of this passage is that the Franks represented the Byzantine Empire.

A Chronology of the First Crusade from Its Roots to Its Chroniclers (325–1108)

325 Constantine restores Jerusalem as a Christian city.

335 Church of the Holy Sepulcher completed.

610 Prophet Muhammad has his first vision, marking the beginning of Islam.

621 Muhammad's Night Journey takes him from Mecca to Jerusalem and then to heaven.

632 Muhammad dies.

637 Caliph Umar conquers Jerusalem and makes it a Muslim capital.

687–691 Dome of the Rock in Jerusalem constructed.

1009 Fatimid caliph al-Hakim orders the destruction of the Church of the Holy Sepulcher.

1028 Fatimid caliph Ali az-Zahir authorizes the reconstruction of the Church of the Holy Sepulcher.

1055 Seljuk Turks establish themselves as the rulers of Baghdad.

1064–1065 Great German Pilgrimage to Jerusalem.

1071 Battle of Manzikert, victory of Seljuk Turks over Byzantine Greeks.

1073 Seljuk Turks capture Jerusalem from the Fatimid Caliphate.

1084 Seljuk Turks capture Antioch from the Byzantine Empire.

1095 *March 1–7* Council of Piacenza.

November 18–28 Council of Clermont.

1096 *March 8* Armies of Peter the Hermit begin the journey to Jerusalem.

May 3–27 Jews persecuted at Speyer, Worms, and finally Mainz.

August–September Princely crusading armies begin departures for Jerusalem.

August 1 Peter the Hermit's armies arrive at Constantinople.

October 21–22 Turks of Nicaea massacre the followers of Peter the Hermit.

December 23 Armies of Godfrey of Bouillon reach Constantinople.

1097 *April 10* Bohemond arrives at Constantinople ahead of his army.

April 21 Raymond of Saint-Gilles arrives at Constantinople ahead of his army.

May 6 Siege of Nicaea begins.

May 14 Robert of Normandy and Stephen of Blois lead final crusading armies to Constantinople.

June 3 All crusading armies rendezvous at Nicaea, where the siege continues.

June 19 Nicaea surrenders to representatives of Emperor Alexius.

July 1 Crusaders defeat an army of Seljuk Turks led by Kilij Arslan.

October 20 Siege of Antioch begins.

December 30 Peter Bartholomew's first vision.

1098 *June 3* Crusaders capture Antioch through the treachery of one of the city's defenders.

June 5 Kerbogah of Mosul besieges Antioch, trapping crusaders inside.

June 14 Discovery of the Holy Lance of Antioch, under Peter Bartholomew's leadership.

June 28 Crusaders defeat Kerbogah's army.

August 1 Bishop Adhémar, spiritual leader of the crusade, dies.

1099 *April 8* Peter Bartholomew undergoes trial by fire.

June 7 Crusaders reach Jerusalem; siege begins.

June 13 First crusader assault on Jerusalem fails.

July 8 Crusaders make solemn procession around Jerusalem in preparation for the final battle.

July 15 Crusaders capture Jerusalem and massacre much of the Muslim garrison.

July 16 Some crusaders massacre Muslim prisoners, whom Tancred had been holding for ransom.

July 17 Crusaders carry out a general massacre of Jerusalem's Muslim population.

ca. 1100 Anonymous *Deeds of the Franks* and chronicle of Raymond of Aguilers completed.

1105 Ali ibn Tahir al-Sulami's *Book of Holy War.*

ca. 1106 Early version of the chronicle of Fulcher of Chartres enters circulation.

ca. 1107 Baudry of Bourgueil, Robert the Monk, and Guibert of Nogent write their crusade chronicles, based primarily on *The Deeds of the Franks.* Albert of Aachen probably begins his chronicle at about the same time.

1108 Ralph of Caen joins Tancred, whose biography he will write, in the Middle East.

Questions for Consideration

1. How different are the Old Testament ideas of holy war from those of the Qur'an?
2. Based on what you have read, what, if anything, did European Christians know about the Muslim religion?
3. Why might crusaders have associated the villains in the prophecies of Pseudo-Methodius with the Seljuk Turks in Syria and Palestine?
4. What made Jerusalem sacred to both Christians and Muslims? How did each culture's view of Jerusalem shape Christian and Muslim authors' presentations of the final battles of the crusade?
5. Why did stories of violence in Jerusalem in 1009 and in 1096 inspire attacks against Jews in Europe?
6. Compare the treatment of Jews in Document 23 with the treatment of Muslims in Document 50. How do you explain the similarities?
7. What insights, if any, do the stories of the great German pilgrimage of 1064 provide about the beliefs of the first crusaders?
8. How well did the crusade chroniclers understand Urban II's indulgence, as described in Document 15?
9. Compare the Greek and Arabic historical narrative sources with the Latin Christian ones. What are the fundamental differences in style and in the types of information they sought to convey?
10. The Catholic Church did not begin to define what the crusade was until the end of the twelfth century, although observers on the ground clearly believed that the First Crusade was a special type of war unique to itself. Based on the sources presented here, how would you define a crusade?
11. A number of factors help to explain the crusaders' conquest of Jerusalem—which seems, on the face of it, improbable. These include Western military tactics, political disunity in the Islamic world, and the ideologies of warfare characteristic of the various factions involved. How do you weigh the relative importance of these factors based on the sources you have read?

12. What made Peter Bartholomew's visions about the Holy Lance believable to the army? Why did the soldiers ultimately turn against him?
13. How do you interpret the symbolism of Christ's five wounds in Document 41?
14. Compare Documents 21, 42, and 48. What characteristics emerge from Ralph of Caen's presentation of his hero, Tancred? Do they together constitute a consistent psychological portrait?
15. Compare al-Sulami's conception of jihad with the crusaders' ideas of holy war. How well did al-Sulami understand the crusade?
16. Based on what you have read from Arabic sources, why was al-Sulami's call for concerted holy war against the crusaders not more immediately successful?
17. Compare the outcomes of the battle for Nicaea and the battle for Jerusalem. What best explains the different results of these battles?
18. The writers of some of our sources (the anonymous author of *The Deeds of the Franks*, Raymond of Aguilers, and Fulcher of Chartres) were clerics who participated in the crusade. Others (Baudry of Bourgueil, Guibert of Nogent, Robert the Monk, and Albert of Aachen) were churchmen who never traveled to the Middle East. At least one writer (Ralph of Caen) was a priest who did not participate in the crusade but who did emigrate to the crusader settlements and knew many of the participants well. Are there significant differences in the ways these writers approached their subject? And might these differences have grown out of their different levels of connection to the Holy Land and the crusade, or perhaps out of other aspects of their particular backgrounds?
19. Does a coherent historical memory of the crusade emerge from our Latin (Western) sources?

Selected Bibliography

PRIMARY SOURCES FOR THE FIRST CRUSADE IN TRANSLATION

Abū Ya'lá Ḥamzah ibn Asad Ibn al-Qalānisī. *The Damascus Chronicle of the Crusades.* Translated by H. A. R. Gibb. London: Luzac, 1932.

Albert of Aachen. *Historia Ierosolimitana, History of the Journey to Jerusalem.* Edited and translated by Susan B. Edgington. Oxford: Clarendon Press, 2007.

Anna Comnena. *The Alexiad.* Translated by E. R. A. Sewter. Edited by Peter Frankopan. London: Penguin Classics, 2009.

Chanson d'Antioche: An Old French Account of the First Crusade. Translated by Susan B. Edgington and Carol Sweetenham. Burlington, Vt.: Ashgate, 2011.

The Deeds of the Franks and the Other Pilgrims to Jerusalem. Edited and translated by Rosalind Hill. London: T. Nelson, 1962.

Fulcher of Chartres. *A History of the Expedition to Jerusalem, 1095–1127.* Translated by Frances Rita Ryan. Knoxville: University of Tennessee Press, 1969.

Gilo of Paris. *Historia vie Hierosolimitane.* Edited and translated by C. W. Grocock and J. E. Siberry. Oxford: Clarendon Press, 1997.

Guibert of Nogent. *The Deeds of God through the Franks: A Translation of Guibert de Nogent's* Gesta Dei per Francos. Translated by Robert Levine. Woodbridge, U.K.: Boydell Press, 1997.

Ibn al-Athir. *The Chronicle of Ibn al-Athir for the Crusading Period from al-Kamil fi'l-Ta'rikh.* Translated by D. S. Richards. 3 vols. Burlington, Vt.: Ashgate, 2005–2008.

Peter Tudebode. *Historia de Hierosolymitano itinere.* Translated by John Hugh Hill and Laurita Littleton Hill. Philadelphia: American Philosophical Society, 1974.

Ralph of Caen. *The* Gesta Tancredi *of Ralph of Caen.* Translated by Bernard S. Bachrach and David S. Bachrach. Burlington, Vt.: Ashgate, 2005.

Raymond of Aguilers. *Historia Francorum Qui Ceperunt Iherusalem.* Translated by John Hugh Hill and Laurita Littleton Hill. Philadelphia: American Philosophical Society, 1968.

Robert the Monk. *Robert the Monk's History of the First Crusade: Historia Hierosolimitana*. Translated by Carol Sweetenham. Burlington, Vt.: Ashgate, 2005.

William of Tyre. *A History of Deeds Done beyond the Sea*. Translated by Emily Atwater Babcock and A. C. Krey. 2 vols. New York: Columbia University Press, 1943.

GENERAL HISTORIES OF THE CRUSADES

Asbridge, Thomas. *The Crusades: The Authoritative History of the War for the Holy Land*. New York: HarperCollins, 2010.

Chazan, Robert. *European Jewry and the First Crusade*. Berkeley: University of California Press, 1987.

Madden, Thomas F. *The New Concise History of the Crusades*. Lanham, Md.: Rowman and Littlefield, 2005.

Phillips, Jonathan. *Holy Warriors: A Modern History of the Crusades*. New York: Random House, 2010.

Tyerman, Christopher. *God's War: A New History of the Crusades*. Cambridge, Mass.: Harvard University Press, 2006.

HISTORIES OF THE FIRST CRUSADE

Asbridge, Thomas. *The First Crusade: A New History*. Oxford: Oxford University Press, 2004.

France, John. *Victory in the East: A Military History of the First Crusade*. Cambridge, U.K.: Cambridge University Press, 1994.

Frankopan, Peter. *The First Crusade: The Call from the East*. Cambridge, Mass.: Belknap Press of Harvard University Press, 2012.

Riley-Smith, Jonathan. *The First Crusade and the Idea of Crusading*. London: Athlone, 1986.

Rubenstein, Jay. *Armies of Heaven: The First Crusade and the Quest for Apocalypse*. New York: Basic Books, 2011.

CRUSADER MOTIVATION AND CRUSADER CULTURE

Bull, Marcus. *Knightly Piety and the Lay Response to the First Crusade: The Limousin and Gascony, c. 970–c. 1130*. Oxford: Oxford University Press, 1993.

Cole, Penny. *The Preaching of the Crusades to the Holy Land*. Cambridge, Mass.: Medieval Academy of America, 1991.

Edgington, Susan B., and Sarah Lambert, eds. *Gendering the Crusades*. New York: Columbia University Press, 2002.

Erdmann, Carl. *The Origin of the Idea of Crusade*. Translated by Marshall W. Baldwin and Walter Goffart. Princeton, N.J.: Princeton University Press, 1977.

Morris, Colin. "Policy and Visions: The Case of the Holy Lance at Antioch." In *War and Government in the Middle Ages: Essays in Honour of J. O. Prestwich*, edited by J. Gillingham and J. C. Holt, 33–45. Woodbridge, U.K.: Boydell Press, 1984.

Purkis, William J. *Crusading Spirituality in the Holy Land and Iberia, c. 1095–c. 1187*. Woodbridge, U.K.: Boydell Press, 2008.

Riley-Smith, Jonathan. *The First Crusaders, 1095–1131*. Cambridge, U.K.: Cambridge University Press, 1997.

Smith, Katherine Allen. *War and the Making of Medieval Monastic Culture*. Woodbridge, U.K.: Boydell Press, 2011.

Throop, Susanna A. *Crusading as an Act of Vengeance, 1095–1216*. Burlington, Vt.: Ashgate, 2011.

HOLY WAR, JUST WAR, AND CRUSADER VIOLENCE

Brundage, James A. *Medieval Canon Law and the Crusader*. Madison: University of Wisconsin Press, 1969.

Head, Thomas, and Richard Landes, eds. *The Peace of God: Social Violence and Religious Response in France around the Year 1000*. Ithaca, N.Y.: Cornell University Press, 1992.

Kedar, Benjamin Z. "The Jerusalem Massacres of July 1099 in the Western Historiography of the Crusades." *Crusades* 3 (2004): 15–76.

Mastnak, Tomaž. *Crusading Peace: Christendom, the Muslim World, and Western Political Order*. Berkeley: University of California Press, 2002.

Russell, Frederick. *The Just War in the Middle Ages*. Cambridge, U.K.: Cambridge University Press, 1975.

ISLAM AND THE CRUSADES

Bonner, Michael. *Jihad in Islamic History: Doctrines and Practice*. Princeton, N.J.: Princeton University Press, 2006.

Cobb, Paul M. *The Race for Paradise: An Islamic History of the Crusades*. Oxford: Oxford University Press, 2014.

Daniel, Norman. *Heroes and Saracens: An Interpretation of the* Chansons de Geste. Edinburgh: Edinburgh University Press, 1984.

Gabrieli, Francesco. *Arab Historians of the Crusades*. Translated by E. J. Costello. Berkeley: University of California Press, 1984.

Hillenbrand, Carole. *The Crusades: Islamic Perspectives*. Edinburgh: Edinburgh University Press, 1999.

Kedar, Benjamin Z. *Crusade and Mission: European Approaches toward Muslims*. Princeton, N.J.: Princeton University Press, 1984.

Tolan, John V. *Saracens: Islam in the Medieval European Imagination*. New York: Columbia University Press, 2002.

JERUSALEM IN MEDIEVAL HISTORY

Boas, Adrian J. *Jerusalem in the Time of the Crusades*. New York: Routledge, 2001.

Hamilton, Bernard. "The Impact of Crusader Jerusalem on Western Christendom." *Catholic History Review* 80 (1994): 695–713.

Morris, Colin. *The Sepulchre of Christ and the Medieval West: From the Beginning to 1600*. Oxford: Oxford University Press, 2005.

Schein, Sylvia. *Gateway to the Heavenly City: Crusader Jerusalem and the Catholic West, 1099–1187*. Burlington, Vt.: Ashgate, 2005.

MEDIEVAL APOCALYPTIC THOUGHT

Cohn, Norman. *The Pursuit of the Millennium*. London: Secker and Warberg, 1957.

Emmerson, Richard K., and Bernard McGinn, eds. *The Apocalypse in the Middle Ages*. Ithaca, N.Y.: Cornell University Press, 1992.

Landes, Richard. "The Fear of an Apocalyptic Year 1000: Augustinian Historiography, Medieval and Modern." *Speculum* 75 (2000): 97–145.

McGinn, Bernard, ed. *Visions of the End: Apocalyptic Traditions in the Middle Ages*. New York: Columbia University Press, 1998.

Whalen, Brett. *Dominion of God: Christendom and Apocalypse in the Middle Ages*. Cambridge, Mass.: Harvard University Press, 2009.

Acknowledgments (*continued from p. iv*)

Document 6. From Naṣer-e Khosraw, *Book of Travels* (Safarnāma), translated by W. M. Thackston, Jr. (Albany, N.Y.: Bibliotheca Persica, 1986). Copyright © 1986 The Persian Heritage Foundation. Used by permission of The Persian Heritage Foundation.

Document 11. From Paul E. Walker, *Caliph of Cairo: Al-Hakim bi-Amr Allah, 996–1021,* by Paul E. Walker (Cairo: The American University in Cairo Press, 2009). Used by permission of the publisher.

Document 23. From *European Jewry and the First Crusade,* translated by Robert Chazan (Berkeley: University of California Press, 1987). Copyright © 1987 by the Regents of the University of California. Published by the University of California Press. Used by permission of the publisher.

Document 24. From *The Alexiad of Anna Comnena,* translated by E. R. A. Sewter (Penguin Classics, 1969), pages 311–13. Copyright © E. R. A. Sewter, 1969. Reproduced by permission of Penguin Books Ltd.

Document 27. From *The Alexiad of Anna Comnena,* translated by E. R. A. Sewter (Penguin Classics, 1969), pages 326–30. Copyright © E. R. A. Sewter, 1969. Reproduced by permission of Penguin Books Ltd.

Document 34. From *The Chronicle of Ibn al-Athir for the Crusading Period from al-Kamil fi'l-Ta'rikh,* Part 1, translated by D. S. Richards. (Surrey, U.K.: Ashgate Publishing). Copyright © D. S. Richards, 2005. Used by permission of the publisher.

Document 40. From *The Chronicle of Ibn al-Athir for the Crusading Period from al-Kamil fi'l-Ta'rikh,* Part 1, translated by D. S. Richards. (Surrey, U.K.: Ashgate Publishing). Copyright © D. S. Richards, 2005. Used by permission of the publisher.

Document 49. From *The Chronicle of Ibn al-Athir for the Crusading Period from al-Kamil fi'l-Ta'rikh,* Part 1, translated by D. S. Richards. (Surrey, U.K.: Ashgate Publishing). Copyright © D. S. Richards, 2005. Used by permission of the publisher.

Document 53. English translation based on Emmanuel Sivan, "La genèse de la contre-croisade: Un traité damasquin du début du XIIe siècle," *Journal Asiatique* 254 (1966). Used by permission.

Index